# Teaching the Ethical Foundations of Economics

Jonathan B. Wight

John S. Morton

This publication was made possible by the generous

support of the John Templeton Foundation

**NCEE**

**National Council on Economic Education**

# Authors

Project Directors and Lead Authors

**Jonathan B. Wight**
University of Richmond

**John S. Morton**
Arizona Council on Economic Education

Authors

**Martin Calkins**
University of Massachusetts-Boston

**Sally Finch**
Westminster Schools, Atlanta

**Daniel M. Hausman**
University of Wisconsin-Madison

**Mark C. Schug**
University of Wisconsin-Milwaukee

**Charles Wilber**
University of Notre Dame

**William C. Wood**
James Madison University

Project Editor
**Melinda Patterson Grenier**

Design
**Karl Hartig**

ISBN          1-56183-648-6          5 4 3 2 1

# Contents

Acknowledgments                                                                        iv

Foreword                                                                                v

Introduction:   Why Ethics Is Important to Economics                                  vii

                A User's Guide to These Lessons                                         ix

Lesson 1        Does Science Need Ethics?                                                1

Lesson 2        What Is the Difference Between Self-Interest and Greed?                 17

Lesson 3        Do Markets Need Ethical Standards?                                      29

Lesson 4        Do Markets Make Us More Moral?                                          45

Lesson 5        What Are the Moral Limits of Markets?                                   61

Lesson 6        What Should We Do About Sweatshops?                                     81

Lesson 7        Should We Allow a Market for Transplant Organs?                        107

Lesson 8        Is Efficiency an Ethical Concept?                                      127

Lesson 9        Do Businesses Have a Social Responsibility?                            145

Lesson 10       What Is Economic Justice?                                              161

Test Bank                                                                              177

Glossary of Terms                                                                      185

# Acknowledgments

## External Reviewers

**Thomas W. Dunfee**
The Wharton School
University of Pennsylvania

**Dwight R. Lee**
The Terry College of Business
University of Georgia

## Field-Test Teachers

**Fred Cole**
Marquette Senior High School
Marquette, Mich.

**Mark DeCourcy**
Sandy Creek High School
Tyrone, Ga.

**Mark Cywinski**
Brown Deer High School
Brown Deer, Wisc.

**Elaine M. Ellsmore**
Pleasant Valley High School
Chico, Calif.

**Donald Fortner**
Munster High School
Munster, Ind.

**Thomas J. Fugate**
Homestead High School
Mequon, Wisc.

**Judy Haley**
Pinetree High School
Longview, Texas

**Brett Hardin**
Campbell High School
Atlanta, Ga.

**Marc Hefke**
Marquette Senior High School
Marquette, Mich.

**Shannon Joyner**
Corona del Sol High School
Tempe, Ariz.

**Jane Tuohey Keller**
The Steward School
Richmond, Va.

**Michael D. Langley**
College Park High School
Pleasant Hill, Calif.

**Sally Meek**
Plano West Senior High
School
Plano, Texas

**Delisse Metcalf**
Chandler High School
Chandler, Ariz.

**Gary Petmecky**
Parkview High School
Snellville, Ga.

**Latricia Piotrowski**
Hebron High School
Carrollton, Texas

**Mary Stevenson**
Marquette Senior High School
Marquette, Mich.

**Robert Wedge**
Collegiate School
Richmond, Va.

**Keith White**
Peoria High School
Peoria, Ariz.

**Petar Zegura**
Moreau Catholic High School
Hayward, Calif.

# Foreword

The National Council on Economic Education is proud to present these innovative instructional materials that show the important role ethics and character play in a market economy and how, in turn, markets influence ethical behavior. These 10 lessons reintroduce an ethical dimension to economics in the tradition of Adam Smith, who believed ethical considerations were central to life.

The lessons do more than illustrate how ethical conduct improves an economy. They actively involve the students through simulations, group decision making, problem solving, classroom demonstrations and role playing. The lessons encourage students to think critically about ethical dilemmas.

Many people made this vision of introducing ethics into the high school curriculum a reality. Jonathan Wight and John Morton led this effort from the initial ideas to the final publication. The dedication, insight and creativity of the author team will be apparent when teachers use the lessons in their classrooms. Thomas Dunfee and Dwight Lee provided valuable external reviews of the manuscript, and 20 teachers from several states field-tested the lessons and made suggestions that greatly improved them.

Finally, without the visionary philanthropy of the John Templeton Foundation, none of this would be possible.

**Robert F. Duvall**, Ph.D.
President and Chief Executive Officer
National Council on Economic Education

# Introduction
# Why Ethics Is Important to Economics

If economics involves the search for truth about the world — why the price of gasoline rises or why the unemployment rate falls — aren't such scientific matters immune to personal ideals of right and wrong?

These lessons provide opportunities for teachers and their students to explore this question. Our thesis is that ethics — consideration of right and wrong — does matter to economics. Economics grapples with how societies deal with limited resources and how exchange plays a part in this process. Why do strangers return lost wallets? Why are doctors concerned about their patients' best interests? Why does fairness seem to produce higher economic returns than greed? Ethical values and moral frameworks permeate exchange.

The study of ethics in economic life is growing exponentially. This is partly because of recent scandals at major energy, health-care and other firms. These scandals highlight the destructive power a few immoral managers can wreak on a company and on the market. These same moral failings also cause problems in government and nonprofit sectors of the economy.

However, the renewed interest in ethics actually began after the fall of the Soviet Union in 1991, when it became clear that simply unleashing markets, without first creating a workable system of justice, would fail to create conditions for social development. Justice matters to economic life in many ways. Courts and judges are needed to enforce contracts and uphold private-property rights. But formal justice pales in comparison with informal justice: the moral code every citizen carries around in his or her head while going about daily life as an employee, business owner and customer.

As economists, we need to understand how ethical conduct reduces transaction costs, enhances productivity and creates the social capital that lubricates exchange. The lessons in this book propose that certain absolute ethical standards play an important role in economic life. Perhaps for this reason parents and teachers struggle to develop the character of young people in their charge. Holding students accountable helps them to understand their duties to family, community and nation, just as learning self-control provides a foundation for achievement and personal fulfillment.

Finally, economists play an important role in trying to improve society. Normative economics examines the costs and benefits of alternative policies. Deciding among these alternatives requires people to rank goals, and their rankings are determined by ethical values. While economists typically examine only consequences, they are mistaken in judging that only consequences matter. Most religious and philosophical traditions ask, "Do the ends justify the means?" and "Are there duties that people should uphold, regardless of consequences?" Some people might also ask, "Would the proposed policy help or hurt the development of virtue in our community?" These questions are not distractions in society — or in an economics class. Rather, they encourage people to exercise their moral imaginations and develop an analytical perspective, which will enhance students' capabilities in a complex world.

These 10 lessons pose provocative questions about sweatshop labor, the sale of human organs, efficiency and equity in health care, the meaning of justice, the morality of markets and the moral limitations of markets. They allow the students to explore important issues in various engaging ways, often through interactive exercises. Ultimately, these lessons ask the students to develop the critical-thinking skills necessary to explore economic and public-policy issues within a wider moral context. It asks them, in short, to become leaders.

**Jonathan B. Wight**
University of Richmond

# Introduction
# A User's Guide to These Lessons

*Teaching the Ethical Foundations of Economics* may sound intimidating, but, in fact, these 10 lessons are highly accessible to high school teachers and their students. The lessons actively engage the students through simulations, problem solving, group decision making, classroom demonstrations and more. Most importantly, the students must think critically about ethical issues and understand why ideas of right and wrong are vital to economic decision making. The issues discussed in these lessons should grab the students' interest.

The following questions and answers provide some insights on ways to use these lessons effectively.

## 1. How difficult are the economic concepts in the lessons?

The lessons incorporate many economic concepts, which are fully explained. Only one lesson has a graph: a supply and demand graph illustrating a price ceiling. These lessons can be used in government, history, business education and international studies classes in addition to economics classes.

## 2. How difficult are the ethics concepts in the lessons?

Because the study of ethics is so often ignored in high school classes, the ethical concepts will be new to most students. As with the economics concepts, the ethics concepts are developed within the context of each lesson. The lessons emphasize three ethical theories that people use to guide their actions:

• The outcomes-based theory of ethics maintains that the best action is the one that produces the best consequences.

• Duty-based ethics focuses on a set of ethical principles, duties or rules to guide actions.

• Virtue-based ethics emphasizes the personal qualities that enable us to do the right things that good people would do. These qualities include honesty, integrity, courage, concern for others and loyalty. The students apply

these theories as they think critically about ethical dilemmas.

## 3. How do the lessons actively engage the students?

Several lessons simulate behavior before the students analyze that behavior. For example, in Lesson 2 the students play the Ultimatum Game to see the difference between self-interest and greed. In Lesson 3 the students assume the roles of doctors and patients to see how enlightened self-interest, duty and virtue improve economic efficiency. In Lesson 5 the students must determine how to allocate a scarce good, while in Lesson 8 they must make life-and-death decisions about how to allocate a life-saving serum.

The lessons emphasize critical thinking and decision making. In Lesson 7, for example, the students must choose one of four policies for allocating kidneys available for transplants. In Lesson 9 the students must take a stand on the social responsibility of business. In Lesson 10 the students play the Veil of Ignorance game, first choosing policies based on self-interest and then choosing again when they do not know what their self-interest is.

## 4. Do I need to use all the lessons?

Each lesson stands on its own and is not dependent on concepts developed in the other lessons. Nevertheless, certain themes carry across many of the lessons.

## 5. Do I need to spend a lot of time preparing to teach these lessons?

Each lesson is complete; all of the Activities, Visuals and other materials are incorporated into the lessons.

## 6. Can I use these lessons to teach national and state economics standards?

Each lesson covers a specific Voluntary National Content Standard in Economics, and most lessons contain more than one standard. Because many state economics standards are based on the national standards, many lessons also teach the state standards. These lessons will help students understand why ethics and economics go together.

## 7. What outcomes can I expect from using these lessons?

The lessons enrich the students' understanding of real-world issues. Public-policy choices require people to combine economic analysis with normative evaluations, including ethical considerations. When the students can see this larger picture, their critical-thinking skills are enhanced.

## 8. How do I assess whether the students have really learned something from these lessons?

Each lesson has three multiple-choice questions and two essay questions that you can use to assess student learning. The questions with answers are provided in the lessons, and the questions without answers are in an appendix so you can copy them for the students.

**John S. Morton**
Arizona Council on Economic Education

# Lesson 1 - Does Science Need Ethics?

*The students discover how a rabbit and a duck illustrate the way ethical judgments affect economic analysis.*

## OVERVIEW

### Economics

Positive economics is the study of the economy as it currently exists (analysis of facts). Normative economics requires people to make judgments about the way the world ought to be (values). The division between positive and normative economics is not precise, however, because values play a critical role in the selection, collection and analysis of information. Understanding the role of ethics in science can improve self-awareness and impartiality in economic investigations.

### Ethics

In conducting positive economic research, economists must make choices: what to study, what type of facts to collect, how many facts to collect and the definition of terms. Values play a role in all these decisions. For example, scientists generally believe the "best" model is the one that can explain the facts in the simplest manner. This means they must make a judgment about how to rate alternative models. Additionally, researchers are expected to tell the truth about their findings, not falsify or withhold them. Ethics contributes to the scientific process.

## LESSON DESCRIPTION

In this lesson the students see how biases may enter into the discovery of facts. Then they follow the progress of an economic researcher as she carries out a positive economic analysis. Finally, they come to appreciate that ethical judgments are central to scientific research, including economic analysis.

## CONCEPTS

Economic model
Facts
Fiduciary duty
Ideology
Moral hazard
Normative economics
Positive economics
Values

## CONTENT STANDARDS

1. Productive resources are limited. Therefore, people cannot have all the goods and services they want; as a result, they must choose some things and give up others.

2. Effective decision making requires comparing the additional costs of alternatives with the additional benefits. Most choices involve doing a little more or a little less of something; few choices are all-or-nothing decisions.

4. People respond predictably to positive and negative incentives.

## OBJECTIVES

The students will:
1. Recognize that positive economics relies on ethical assumptions and considerations.

2. Experience how definitions and the collecting of facts come bundled with ethical judgments.

3. Describe why ethical conduct is essential to the scientific process.

## TIME REQUIRED

45 minutes

## MATERIALS

1. Visuals 1.1 and 1.2

2. One copy of Activity 1.1 for half the students in the class; one copy of Activity 1.2 for the other half

3. One copy of Activity 1.3 for each student

## PROCEDURE

1. Tell the students this lesson illustrates how economists select research projects, gather data, analyze evidence and report the results. The lesson reveals how value judgments and ethical conduct are central to the advancement of science, including a social science such as economics.

2. The first part of this lesson is meant to surprise and engage the students as they see how two groups can use the same information to arrive at very different *facts*. Divide the class into groups of four to five students. Place half the groups on the left side of the room (A Groups). Place the other half on the right (B Groups). Explain that each group is a team of field researchers gathering evidence for a scientific study. Give each student in the A Groups a copy of Activity 1.1, and give each student in the B Groups a copy of Activity 1.2.

3. Allow the students a few minutes to work independently through the questions on the Activities. Then give the groups a few minutes to discuss the questions. Ask the groups to reach consensus on the answer to each question.

4. Ask the students if everyone in their group initially answered the questions the same way. Tell the students you're curious to know their individual answers. Display Visual 1.1. Ask them to raise their hands in response to the questions. Record the totals in the columns on the left side of the Visual. Don't let the students discuss their answers.
   **Question 1:** How many students in the A Groups chose carrots? How many chose minnows? How many students in the B Groups chose carrots? How many chose minnows?
   **Question 2A:** How many students in the A Groups chose 20 years? 50 years? 80 years? How many students in the B Groups chose 20 years? 50 years? 80 years?
   **Question 2B:** How many students in the A Groups chose down? How many chose to the side? How many students in the B Groups chose down? How many chose to the side?
   **Question 3:** How many students in the A Groups chose very good? Good? Poor? Very poor? How many students in the B Groups chose very good? Good? Poor? Very poor?
   **Question 4:** How many students in the A Groups chose more? How many chose less? How many students in the B Groups chose more? How many chose less?

5. Ask one representative from each group to give the group's consensus answer for each question. Record the answers in the columns on the right side of the Visual.

6. Ask the class why they think there was disagreement about the answers among the individual students and the groups. *Accept all answers, and then tell the*

*students the questions are worded in a biased way that influences the answers.*

7.  Display Visual 1.2. Help the students appreciate the "ah-ha factor" in this activity by discussing the biases in the questions. Ask the students if they would have answered differently if the questions had been posed differently. *Most will probably say that they would have answered the questions differently. Bring out the key point that different perceptions affect research.*

8.  Ask the students, "What are the implications of this for economic research?" Bring out these key points during the discussion:
    • *Preconceptions provide the context for understanding economic and other events. People often see what they expect to see and ignore information that contradicts their preconceptions. Focus on duck vs. rabbit, young vs. elderly, 20 percent vs. 50 percent vs. 80 percent and payment vs. avoidance.*
    • *If there is ambiguity, people tend to interpret based on expectations. For example, children tested on Easter Sunday are more likely to see the animal in Question 1 as a rabbit, compared with children tested six months later. (P. Brugger and S. Brugger, "The Easter Bunny in October: Is It Disguised as a Duck?" Perceptual & Motor Skills 76, 1993, 577-578)*
    • *"Facts" are thus often influenced by biases or ethical judgments. Reality can depend on what someone expects to see. For science to advance, researchers must recognize their biases and be as objective as possible.*
    • *Economic definitions have ethical implications for people's lives.*
    • *Knowledge and interpretation of facts have an ethical impact on people's behavior.*

9.  Tell the students that they will now see how these issues play a role in science.

Explain that economics is a branch of the social sciences, which have goals similar to the goals of the natural sciences. Social-science goals are different, however, because they focus on human behavior in groups. The students will follow along as a researcher goes through the steps of an economic investigation. Distribute a copy of Activity 1.3 to each student. Ask them to read "Maria's Research Project" and write the answers to the questions. Discuss the answers with the class.

**Question 1:** What do economists call the study of the way the world actually works? What do economists call the study of policies to make the world a better place? *Positive economics is the study of how the world actually works (facts and theories that explain the facts). The gross domestic product, the unemployment rate, the price of milk and the trade deficit are all facts that positive economists study and explain. Normative economics involves an analysis of the way things ought to be (ethical or value judgments about "good" and "bad" policies).*

**Question 2:** Which of the following statements relies on positive analysis and which relies on normative analysis? How do you know?
   **A.** The economy grew 3 percent last year. *Positive analysis (a statement of fact)*
   **B.** The government should take action to help the economy grow faster than 3 percent next year. *Normative analysis (involves a value judgment that this outcome is preferable). Normative statements often include the words "ought" or "should."*

**Question 3:** How is Maria's choice of career affected by her ethical beliefs? What value judgments did Maria make in picking unemployment as her subject to study? *Maria would like to help make the world a better place and believes that as an economist, she can discover ways to do so. She decides to specialize in unemployment because she* *remembers the painful times during her childhood when her father was unemployed.*

**Question 4:** Do Maria's, Jenny's and Robert's perceptions of reality depend on what they expect to see? Do people tend to ignore information that contradicts their preconceptions? *How we perceive an outside reality is partly a function of our inside mental activity. Thus, ideology and our acquaintance with prior random information can bias the identification and collection of what we call "facts." Investigators often "see" what their prescientific vision leads them to expect to see and ignore information that contradicts their preconceptions.*

*According to one study, "once a belief or expectation is found, especially one that resolves uncomfortable uncertainty, it biases the observer to notice new information that confirms the belief and to discount evidence to the contrary. This self-perpetuating mechanism consolidates the original error and builds up an overconfidence in which the arguments of opponents are seen as too fragmentary to undo the adopted belief." (http://skepdic. com/forer.html)*

**Question 5:** Why do economists include only the most essential variables in an economic model? *An economic model acts like a road map. A map shows the essential highways leading from City A to City B. It does not show all the smaller roads that intersect. By focusing only on the most important variables, an economic model provides a clearer view of the factors that affect economic behavior.*

**Question 6:** Do economists get facts for free? If not, what factors determine why economists collect some facts and not others? *Economic data come from a variety of sources, some private (teen-spending statistics collected by a research firm) and some public (Commerce Department estimates of*

*output and inflation). Either way, it is costly to collect information. The Labor Department can save significant amounts of money by surveying "representative families" rather than "all families" to estimate unemployment. Survey estimates always involve a margin of error. To make a better estimate would cost more (for example, by surveying a larger sample). Are better estimates worth the expense? This is a normative judgment. From the taxpayers' perspective, any money spent on refining the estimate of the unemployment rate comes at the expense of getting a better estimate of the inflation rate or at the expense of higher taxes. There's no free lunch. A decision about which data to collect (and of what quality) is a value decision about what is most important.*

**Question 7:** Does the way Maria phrases her survey questions influence the answers people give her? If so, what are the implications of this for using surveys to measure economic data? *Behavioral economists have identified many instances in which people give inconsistent and contradictory answers to essentially the same questions. Surveyors should take this "irrationality" into consideration when they develop research questions.*

**Question 8:** True or false and why? People don't ever make value judgments in carrying out good science. *False. Scientific investigations require ethical choices.*

**Question 9:** Malcolm is researching a new drug, and his results show that it is not effective. He is suddenly offered a well-paying job with the company that makes the drug — but only if he suppresses his results. What is this situation called? *A moral hazard, because Malcolm has an economic interest to do something unethical. Falsifying or suppressing results of scientific investigations can cause financial or physical harm to innocent people.*

**Question 10:** For science to advance, what absolute moral standards should all researchers obey? *Some absolute moral standards for researchers are honesty, integrity, fair-mindedness, courage, empathy and intellectual autonomy.*

**Question 11:** Why is ethical conduct so important for Maria's research? *A researcher's ethical beliefs help determine the way she asks the questions, interprets the answers and uses the research. Maria will do better work if she is conscious of the value choices she makes in defining, collecting and analyzing data. Maria must be careful to avoid moral hazards such as suppressing results that go against her opinions or that would displease her employer or her father.*

## CLOSURE

10. Review the ways in which scientific research requires ethical choices. Ask the students what ethical behaviors are required of researchers for scientific research to be effective. *Researchers should be aware that everyone approaches problems from a particular worldview and that this creates possible sources of inspiration but also of bias. Researchers should therefore strive to be as impartial as possible when they do positive economic analysis and to obey absolute moral standards of behavior regarding honesty, integrity, fair-mindedness and intellectual autonomy.*

**The bottom line:** Economists will do better work if they are conscious of the ethical choices researchers face, including the choices involved in positive economic research.

## ASSESSMENT

### Multiple-Choice Questions

1.1 Researchers in economics
    A. face ethical issues only in normative economics.
    B. face ethical issues only in positive economics.
    *C. face ethical issues in both positive and normative economics.*
    D. face no ethical issues because economics is a science.

1.2 A moral hazard arises when a researcher
    A. is put in peril from dangerous workplace materials.
    *B. has an economic incentive to behave unethically.*
    C. is in jeopardy from being overly ethical.
    D. cannot behave ethically because of a legal restriction.

1.3 If productive resources are limited, scarcity implies that
    *A. people will collect only the facts they consider most important.*
    B. people will base their collection of facts solely on objective considerations.
    C. all facts are of equal importance to researchers.
    D. researchers don't consider values when they collect facts.

### Essay Questions

1.1 In what ways are facts different from values? In what ways are they related in economic research? *Economists analyze facts to study the economy as it currently exists. They make value judgments about the way the world ought to be. Research into facts often requires funding. Since funding is scarce, researchers must make value judgments to decide which projects are most important. They must identify, collect and analyze facts. The researcher and project funders must make normative judgments about the definition of facts, which facts to collect, how to collect them, how many to collect and how to use them.*

1.2 What absolute moral values are necessary to conduct scientific research? *Science relies on honesty, integrity, courage and fair-mindedness. Progress in science is greatly hindered without these absolute moral values.*

## GOING FURTHER

**Vision:** For a discussion of worldview, see the pathbreaking work by Thomas Kuhn, *The Structure of Scientific Revolutions* (Chicago: University of Chicago Press, 1962).

**Critical Thinking:** Critical thinking is a key attribute of good science. *The Skeptic's Dictionary* (http://skepdic.com) has many items of interest for students, especially a guide to critical thinking (http://www.skepdic.com/essays/haskins.pdf).

**Perception:** For ambiguities of perception, see "Duck-Rabbit Illusion" at *MathWorld* (http://mathworld.wolfram.com/Rabbit-DuckIllusion.html).

**Knowledge and Values:** For an historical view of the facts-versus-values debate going back to Plato, see Henryk Skolimowski, "Knowledge and Values," *Ecologist* 5, no. 1 (January 1975): 2-9.

**Economic Models and Ethical Ramifications:** To learn how the teaching of positive economics can have ethical repercussions, see the widely-cited articles by Robert H. Frank, "Do Economists Make Bad Citizens?" *Journal of Economic Perspectives* 10 (Winter 1996): 187-192; and Robert H. Frank, Thomas D. Gilovich and Dennis T. Regan, "Does Studying Economics Inhibit Cooperation?" *Journal of Economic Perspectives* 7 (Spring 1993): 159-171.

# VISUAL 1.1
# FIELD RESEARCH: COLLECTING THE EVIDENCE

| Students in A Groups | Students in B Groups | | A Groups | B Groups |
|---|---|---|---|---|
| | | **Question 1** | | |
| | | Carrots | | |
| | | Minnows | | |
| | | **Question 2A** | | |
| | | 20 years | | |
| | | 50 years | | |
| | | 80 years | | |
| | | **Question 2B** | | |
| | | Down | | |
| | | To the side | | |
| | | **Question 3** | | |
| | | Very good | | |
| | | Good | | |
| | | Poor | | |
| | | Very poor | | |
| | | **Question 4** | | |
| | | More | | |
| | | Less | | |

# VISUAL 1.2
# FIELD RESEARCH: HOW BIAS AFFECTS PERCEPTION
# GROUP A [GROUP B IN BRACKETS]

Reproduced with permission of authors and publisher from: Brugger, P., and Brugger, S. "The Easter Bunny in October: Is it disguised as a duck?" Perceptual and Motor Skills, 1993, 76, 577-578. (c) Perceptual and Motor Skills 1993

**DIRECTIONS:** Answer these questions by CIRCLING the response you think is best.

**1.** Examine the **duck [rabbit]** in the picture on the left. What does this animal like to eat?

    Carrots from the garden    Minnows from the lake

**2.** Examine the portrait of the **young woman [elderly woman]** in the picture on the right.

    **A.** What is her age?    20 years    50 years    80 years

    **B.** Where is she looking?    Down    To the side

**3.** Your doctor says that you have a **20 percent chance of dying [80 percent chance of surviving]** during a surgical procedure. How would you rate your chance of survival?

    Very good    Good    Poor    Very poor

**4.** An economic study reports that 85 percent of the people in your community **pay their share [avoid paying their share]** of the costs for public projects such as roads and schools. Such **payment [avoidance]** is said to be economically rational. Given this information, are you more or less likely to pay your share of the costs for public projects?

    More    Less

# ACTIVITY 1.1
# FIELD RESEARCH: COLLECTING THE EVIDENCE
# (A GROUPS)

Reproduced with permission of authors and publisher from: Brugger, P., and Brugger, S. "The Easter Bunny in October: Is it disguised as a duck?" Perceptual and Motor Skills, 1993, 76, 577-578. (c) Perceptual and Motor Skills 1993

**DIRECTIONS:** Answer these questions by CIRCLING the response you think is best.

**1.** Examine the duck in the picture on the left. What does this animal like to eat?

 Carrots from the garden    Minnows from the lake

**2.** Examine the portrait of the young woman in the picture on the right.

  **A.** What is her age?    20 years    50 years    80 years

  **B.** Where is she looking?    Down    To the side

**3.** Your doctor says that you have a 20 percent chance of dying during a surgical procedure. How would you rate your chance of survival?

 Very good    Good    Poor    Very poor

**4.** An economic study reports that 85 percent of the people in your community pay their share of the costs for public projects such as roads and schools. Such payment is said to be economically rational. Given this information, are you more or less likely to pay your share of the costs for public projects?

 More    Less

# ACTIVITY 1.2
# FIELD RESEARCH: COLLECTING THE EVIDENCE
# (B GROUPS)

Reproduced with permission of authors and publisher from: Brugger, P., and Brugger, S. "The Easter Bunny in October: Is it disguised as a duck?" Perceptual and Motor Skills, 1993, 76, 577-578. (c) Perceptual and Motor Skills 1993

**DIRECTIONS:** Answer these questions by CIRCLING the response you think is best.

**1.** Examine the rabbit in the picture on the left. What does this animal like to eat?

    Carrots from the garden     Minnows from the lake

**2.** Examine the portrait of the elderly woman in the picture on the right.

    **A.** What is her age?     20 years     50 years     80 years

    **B.** Where is she looking?     Down     To the side

**3.** Your doctor says that you have an 80 percent chance of surviving a surgical procedure. How would you rate your chance of survival?

    Very good     Good     Poor     Very poor

**4.** An economic study reports that 85 percent of the people in your community avoid paying their share of the costs for public projects such as roads and schools. Such avoidance is said to be economically rational. Given this information, are you more or less likely to pay your share of the costs for public projects?

    More     Less

# ACTIVITY 1.3
# MARIA'S RESEARCH PROJECT

In this activity we follow a researcher as she selects an economic topic, builds a model, gathers data to test the model and reports the results.

## Introduction

Maria Smith has decided that she will become an economist. She believes that economics can help her discover important things about the way the world actually works (*positive economics*). She would also like to help make the world a better place (*normative economics*).

## Step I: Picking a Subject for Study (Vision)

When Maria was a child, her father suffered several painful episodes of unemployment during times of economic recession. Maria's initial understanding of economics came from her father's belief that his unemployment was the consequence of employers trying to break the backs of labor unions. This understanding is Maria's *ideology*: the characteristic thinking or beliefs of a particular group, culture or class at a point in time. Ideology — coupled with random knowledge — constitutes the preanalytical worldview or vision that individuals bring to any new study.

Maria decides to specialize within economics to increase her productivity. To choose a specialty, Maria will need to analyze the costs and benefits of different career paths. Maria's analysis is shaped by her value judgment of what she considers most important based on her preanalytical vision and her moral beliefs. For example, Maria would never consider becoming a drug pusher, even if the economic benefits of this career were shown to be highly positive. After some thought, Maria decides to specialize in the study of unemployment and its causes.

## Step II: Perception and Model-Building

After she graduates from college, Maria gets a job at a foundation. Her first project is a study on local unemployment. She decides to drive around her city to get a feel for the problem. She invites her friends Jenny and Robert to ride along. As the trio enters a depressed economic area, they observe a group of men in their early twenties clustered on a street corner. Each researcher applies a different mental model to explain what they observe.

• Maria thinks: "Jobs are just not available for inner-city youth. That's why they're standing around in the middle of the day."

# ACTIVITY 1.3 (continued)
# MARIA'S RESEARCH PROJECT

• Robert, whose father runs a business in the suburbs, thinks: "Jobs are plentiful for people who have a strong work ethic. These kids probably don't want to work."

• Jenny thinks: "One of these men looks familiar. I wonder if he works the night shift at the power plant."

## Step III: Methodology of Data Collection

Maria is now ready to start the formal part of her research on unemployment. But she can't gather any *facts* without first knowing which facts are important to look for. To figure this out, she needs a model or theory to explain the causes of unemployment. Her vision can help her decide what type of *economic model* to build and which data to collect. Models contain only the most essential variables, making assumptions that simplify reality. This is a key part of positive economics. So Maria will make choices and collect the facts that she considers most important or that she thinks can be quantified.

Maria realizes she cannot proceed further until she really pins down what she is trying to measure. She wonders, "What exactly is 'unemployment'?" The Labor Department's official measurement is based on a sampling of households: People 16 years of age and older who are not currently employed but are actively seeking a job are classified as unemployed. Maria realizes that any definition of unemployment requires value judgments. For example, some people become discouraged and give up looking for work; these people would not be counted as unemployed. In addition, from her experience driving through the city with Robert and Jenny, Maria realizes it is expensive in gas and time to survey every family, so she can question only a small sample. She realizes she must make difficult value judgments about how to collect data and how much to collect.

After considering these issues, Maria develops a survey of randomly selected households in her city. One bit of information she'd like to verify from respondents is their reported incomes. But to get this information she might have to lie and pretend to work for the Internal Revenue Service. Maria decides not to gather this information.

## Step IV: Analysis, Dissemination and Impact

In any branch of science, including economics, more than one explanation may exist for the way the world works. Thus, Maria's research on the causes of unemployment may differ from studies done by other researchers. Which theory is correct? For economics to advance, people must subject different theories to external evaluation to

# ACTIVITY 1.3 (continued)
# MARIA'S RESEARCH PROJECT

verify or disprove. The ethical standards for carrying out any debate in economics include first the prime moral commitment to truthfulness. In addition, other *values* play an important role, such as fairness, openness and transparency. For debate to be helpful, there must be a competitive marketplace for ideas.

Suppose Maria's analysis contradicts her father's belief that employers deliberately created unemployment to break the backs of labor unions? Or, what if her results contradict views that benefit the foundation she works for? Maria's narrow economic advantage might be to behave unethically and falsify or suppress her results to gain material rewards from her boss or the praise of her father. This situation is called a *moral hazard*: an economic agent has an economic incentive to behave unethically.

Choosing to behave unethically can have serious negative consequences for others. What if Maria's falsified research leads people to make choices that cause economic loss, injury or death? For science to flourish, people must trust the scientific process. Scientific research thus requires *fiduciary duty*. A fiduciary relationship is one of trust and the expectation of virtuous conduct. For science to work, researchers need the virtues of humility, honesty, courage, empathy, intellectual autonomy, integrity and fair-mindedness. Fortunately, Maria resists the moral-hazard temptation and completes her research in an honest way.

Maria's positive study on local unemployment and her explanation for its causes is published in the *Positive Economic Journal*. After reading it, a senator from her state introduces legislation in Congress to start a public program to train the unemployed.

## Summary

Maria's story highlights the role that ethical choices play in positive scientific research. Impartiality and objectivity are highly desired characteristics for researchers. But perfect impartiality and objectivity are impossible to achieve, and researchers should be aware of how their own values and biases may influence the definition, selection, collection and analysis of information. Economists, like all researchers, have ethical responsibilities. Given this reality, it is clear why certain absolute moral standards are essential for scientific researchers.

Maria's study of positive economics — descriptions or explanations of the world as it is — cannot be perfectly separated from ethical choices she made during her study. Economists will do better work if they are conscious of the ethical choices they make in carrying out positive economics. Value-free science is not possible, nor is it desir-

## ACTIVITY 1.3 (continued)
## MARIA'S RESEARCH PROJECT

able for a number of reasons:
- Choices about what to study involve the researcher's own value judgments.
- Models or theories are often influenced by worldview.
- Facts about the world come bundled with value judgments regarding which and how many facts to collect.
- Knowledge of facts and theories changes a person's view of the world.
- Scientific research requires absolute moral standards.

### Questions

**1.** What do economists call the study of the way the world actually works? What do economists call the study of policies to make the world a better place?

**2.** Which of the following statements relies on positive analysis and which relies on normative analysis? How do you know?
   **A.** The economy grew 3 percent last year.
   **B.** The government should take action to help the economy grow faster than 3 percent next year.

**3.** How is Maria's choice of career affected by her ethical beliefs? What value judgments did Maria make in picking unemployment as her subject to study?

**4.** Do Maria's, Jenny's and Robert's perceptions of reality depend on what they expect to see? Do people tend to ignore information that contradicts their preconceptions?

**5.** Why do economists include only the most essential variables in an economic model?

# ACTIVITY 1.3 (continued)
# MARIA'S RESEARCH PROJECT

**6.** Do economists get facts for free? If not, what factors determine why economists collect some facts and not others?

**7.** Does the way Maria phrases her survey questions influence the answers people give her? If so, what are the implications of this for using surveys to measure economic data?

**8.** True or false and why? People don't ever make value judgments in carrying out good science.

**9.** Malcolm is researching a new drug, and his results show that it is not effective. He is suddenly offered a well-paying job with the company that makes the drug — but only if he suppresses his results. What is this situation called?

**10.** For science to advance, what absolute moral standards should all researchers obey?

**11.** Why is ethical conduct so important for Maria's research?

# Lesson 2 — What Is the Difference Between Self-Interest and Greed?

*The students make, accept and reject ultimatum offers to see how healthy self-interest promotes progress, while uncontrolled self-interest is greed that causes economic harm.*

## OVERVIEW

### Economics

Economics assumes that people rationally seek their own interests. This assumption is the basis of many economic models, including the supply and demand model. In this model, demanders hope to pay a low price and suppliers try to get paid a high price. The result is a price that balances supply and demand. But do people rationally seek their own interests? And does this mean people are basically greedy? Do greedy people prosper in interactions with other people? This lesson explores these questions.

### Ethics

Greed, an excessive desire for more money or goods, is not a virtue. In contrast, prudence (reasonable self-interested behavior) is a virtue. Greed can even be self-defeating: An excessive desire for more money and goods prevents a person from actually receiving more. How do people draw the line between rational self-interest and greed? A challenge for society is to recognize and channel legitimate self-interest while not encouraging greed.

## LESSON DESCRIPTION

In this lesson the students first explore the concepts of greed and self-interest through a class discussion. In pairs they play a famous game in economics and ethics: the Ultimatum Game. One of the pair is a Proposer who suggests how to divide 10 rewards (for example, M&Ms, hard candies, extra-credit points) with a partner, the Responder. The Proposer may suggest keeping from 0 to 10 rewards but must recognize that the Responder may reject highly unequal proposals. If the Responder rejects a proposal, neither participant gets any rewards. The students play four rounds of the game, and then the class discusses the strategies the students employed and the implications of the game for self-interest, greed, altruistic behavior and fairness in business.

## CONCEPTS

Fairness
Greed
Prudence
Rational behavior
Self-interest

## CONTENT STANDARDS

1. Productive resources are limited. Therefore, people cannot have all the goods and services they want; as a result, they must choose some things and give up others.

3. Different methods can be used to allocate goods and services. People, acting individually or collectively through government, must choose which methods to use to allocate different kinds of goods and services.

4. People respond predictably to positive and negative incentives.

## OBJECTIVES

The students will:
1. Explain how self-interest motivates economic behavior.

2. Explain how greed can make an individual less successful.

3. Explain the interaction of self-interest and fairness.

4. Contrast greed with legitimate self-interest.

5. Play the Ultimatum Game, which explores the concepts of greed and self-interest.

## TIME REQUIRED

45 minutes

## MATERIALS

1. Visuals 2.1, 2.2 and 2.3
   (**Note:** Visual 2.2 and Activity 2.1 are the same.)

2. Enough rewards such as M&Ms or hard candies to give each student 20 pieces if the class plays four rounds of the game. (**Note:** If your school does not allow candy in the classroom or if your budget does not allow for candy, students can play for extra-credit points or some other reward.)

3. One copy of Activity 2.1 for each student

## PROCEDURE

1. Explain that the class will explore the difference between self-interest and greed. Ask the students, "What is greed?" *Accept a variety of answers. The fundamental point is that self-interest turns into greed when it is taken "too far" or "to excess." Some students may say that someone's self-interest becomes greed when it hurts others. Others may say that "when I want more, it is self-interest; and when you want more, it is greed."*

2. Display Visual 2.1. Point out that in economics, we often assume that people rationally seek their own interests, but that greed — an excessive desire for more money or goods — is not a virtue.

3. Tell the students that self-interest can produce good outcomes, and then ask, "Why do you expect to receive food when you go to a fast-food restaurant?" *Some students will simply say, "Because you will give them money." Push them to express the self-interest of the restaurant owner, who is in business to make money, or of the employees, whose self-interest led them to work at the restaurant.*

4. Tell the students that the Classical economist Adam Smith made the same point when he wrote (quoted on Visual 2.1): "It is not from the benevolence of the butcher, the brewer, or the baker that we expect our dinner, but from their regard to their own self-interest. We address ourselves, not to their humanity but to their self-love, and never talk to them of our own necessities but of their advantages." Ask: "How might Adam Smith express this point if he were writing today, using modern sellers as examples?" *Smith might say it's not from the benevolence of the gas station owner, the fast-food restaurant manager or the music store clerk that we expect gasoline, food or CDs. Instead it's from their self-interest. They help themselves by learning to serve others.*

5. Distribute one copy of Activity 2.1 to each student, and display Visual 2.2. Using the Visual, tell the students they will play a total of four rounds of the Ultimatum Game. Be sure to tell the students what the rewards will be. Half the class will start the game as Proposers and half as Responders. They will play two rounds, with a new partner for each round. After the second round, they will switch roles: Each Responder becomes a Proposer, and

each Proposer becomes a Responder. The students will play two more rounds — again, with a new partner for each round. Each student will keep a separate score sheet and add up the results after Round 4. Tell the students that they will be disqualified and earn no rewards (candy or extra-credit points) if they start before you say "Go." All rewards will be distributed at the conclusion of the lesson.

6. Now divide the class in half. The group on the left will be Proposers in Round 1, and the group on the right will be Responders. Tell the Proposers that when the game begins, they will pair with a Responder partner (discourage them from selecting a close friend). Remind them that they will find a new partner for each round, and that they will switch roles after the second round. Tell the students when to start the game by saying "Go," and then monitor their game-playing to make sure they are following the rules.

7. At the end of the game, ask the students to add up the number of rewards (candies or extra-credit points) they should get and write the total on their score sheet. Remind the students that you will distribute the rewards at the end of the lesson.

8. Ask these questions to debrief the game:
    A. Did anyone propose a five-and-five division of rewards? Why? *Yes, this is typically the most common proposal; most students will say that five-and-five is a fair proposal. Given the ethic of equal sharing promoted by family life and previous experience in school, the five-and-five proposal is a natural starting point. Some of the students may stay with five-and-five throughout the game.*
    B. Did any Responder reject an offer? Ask Responders why they rejected the offer. *Typically, someone will make a proposal that the Responder rejects. The Responder will justify rejecting the offer, saying it was not fair.*

    C. If you're a Responder and you turn down a proposal of one reward for you and nine for the Proposer, what do you lose? *One reward* What do you gain? *You don't get any rewards, but you have the possible satisfaction of denying nine rewards to an unfair person.*
    D. Why don't Proposers who suggest one candy for the Responder and nine for the Proposer get the most rewards? *The Responders often reject this offer and the Proposer gets nothing. If self-interest becomes greed, as defined by the Responder, the Responder may punish the greedy offer.*
    E. If a one-and-nine division is unfair, is a four-and-six division also unfair? *Accept a variety of answers.*
    F. What is the best strategy for a Proposer who wants the most rewards? *Generally, you will earn more rewards by proposing a division that others consider to be within the bounds of fairness.*
    G. How would the results be different if the players did not know each other and would never meet again? *Accept a variety of answers. Some students who offered five-and-five to their friends might have proposed a more unequal division to a stranger. Even among strangers, however, general ideas of fairness will likely keep Responders from accepting the most unequal allocations, such as one-and-nine.*
    H. What are the limitations of the Ultimatum Game in explaining the difference between self-interest and greed? *The Ultimatum Game is a zero-sum game: If one person gets a piece of candy, the other person does not. There are also negative-sum games and positive-sum games. A person who finds a wallet, takes a few bucks and throws the wallet away may not seem greedy, but most people would find the behavior unacceptable because it is a negative-sum game. On the other hand, a person may receive a billion dollars in profit for discovering a drug that will*

*save millions of lives. This is a posi-tive-sum game. Would your students call this greed? Most market transactions are positive-sum games.*

## CLOSURE

9. Display Visual 2.3. Tell the students that the Ultimatum Game is often played using computers so that neither the Proposer nor the Responder knows whom they are playing with. In this controlled setting, friendship does not influence behavior. Even so, in divisions of $10, the average amount Proposers offer is often about $2.50. Responders will typically reject offers lower than this. Since a rejected offer means no rewards, strict economic logic would say that Responders should accept any offer, even $1. Responders reject such offers because ethical consid-erations are also important: Humans care about justice in addition to wealth. Hence, ethical considerations can affect economic outcomes.

10. Review the main points of the lesson by asking the following questions:

    A. What is the difference between greed and self-interest? *Greed is self-inter-est that has gone too far according to social norms.*

    B. In a market system, do you count on people to provide what you want only because they like helping others? *No, we expect sellers to provide goods and services because it is in their interests. They may also like to help others, but we do not count on this as their pri-mary motivation.*

    C. What does the Ultimatum Game teach you about greed? *Self-interest pushed too far actually works against your own interests. People care about fairness.*

11. Distribute the rewards to the students based on the totals earned in the record sheets.

**The bottom line:** Self-interest may lead peo-ple to make aggressive offers in the market-place, but greed can lead to getting nothing. In the Ultimatum Game and in life, people dislike unfairness and will incur costs to punish it.

## ASSESSMENT

### Multiple-Choice Questions

2.1 A game people use frequently for economic and psychological investigation is called the Ultimatum Game because the game

   A. shows how sellers operate when their product is the best in the market.

   B. is the ultimate in simplicity — that is, the simplest possible two-step game.

   *C. involves a take-it-or-leave-it offer from one person to another.*

   D. shows how disregarding the feelings of others generates profits.

2.2 The difference between rational self-inter-est and greed is that greed

   *A. is excessive, while rational self-interest is a legitimate motivation for people.*

   B. involves money but rational self-interest does not.

   C. exists only in a market system.

   D. concerns only consumers, while rational self-interest concerns consumers and producers.

2.3 Carol buys stock in a new technology company. The company grows, hires more employees and increases profits. Carol sells her stock for much more than she paid for it. This is an example of a

   A. zero-sum game.

   B. negative-sum game.

   *C. positive-sum game.*

   D. ultimatum game.

### Essay Questions

2.1 One winter the weather is unusually cold, and a fuel-oil dealer finds that customers are ordering much more heating oil. If the dealer raises prices in response, is this an example of rational self-interest or greed?

Support your answer. *Some students will characterize raising prices as rational self-interest. Give full credit to an answer that adequately explains this choice; justifications can include the dealer's right to raise prices because the dealer took on the risk of being unable to sell the oil in a mild winter or the mutual rights of the dealer to raise prices and the consumers to shop elsewhere.*

*Give full credit also to a well-supported answer that characterizes the response as greed. Such answers could include the dealer's duty not to take advantage of people who face colder weather through no fault of their own or could focus on the dealer's interests in keeping customers over the long run — sacrificed here to the desire for short-run profit.*

*The situation is more complicated for the students who understand basic economic principles. The opportunity cost of selling fuel oil to one customer is the amount another customer is willing to pay for it. This reflects an ethical feature of market pricing. Market prices motivate us to consider the concerns of others by making us pay an amount for another unit of a product, such as fuel oil, that equals the marginal value others place on it.*

*When others get greater value from a product, they communicate this by being willing to pay higher prices for it. This motivates buyers of the now more-valuable product to use less of it. This process results in sharing the product with others.*

*If the market did not ration fuel oil, the government would have to ration it based on factors other than price. Would this be more or less fair than the market solution? A student who discusses this issue should receive an "A" in economics.*

**2.2** When driving on the freeway, Carl blows his horn repeatedly, tailgates cars and cuts in front of them if he can. Carl explains, "Other drivers are in my way, and I operate the way I do to get to my destination sooner." What benefits does Carl receive from driving in this manner? What costs does he incur? Is Carl showing rational self-interest or greed? Does Carl's strategy always work? *Carl's benefits may include his getting to his destination faster. He incurs costs in the form of a higher probability of causing an accident and being injured, getting a ticket for bad driving, higher insurance costs and the likelihood that other drivers will retaliate against him in "road rage" incidents. Hence, Carl's greedy strategy may backfire. Rational self-interest could lead Carl to control his selfish nature.*

## GOING FURTHER

**Ultimatum Game:** "The Ultimatum Game" by Richard Thaler (*Journal of Economic Perspectives* 2, no. 4, 1988: 195-206) is a useful review article about the game and many experiments that use it.

**Why Do People Value Fairness?** The Ultimatum Game illustrates that people value fairness. Some advanced classes may benefit from going beyond this fact to an extended discussion or an essay assignment on the question, *"Why* do people value fairness?" A useful resource for this exercise is Vernon Smith, "Human Nature: An Economic Perspective," *Daedalus* 133, no. 4 (Fall 2004): 67-76. Student perspectives will vary. Some, following a tradition that goes at least as far back as Adam Smith, will say that fairness is "wired" into human nature. In his *Theory of Moral Sentiments* (Indianapolis: Liberty Fund, 1976, 225), Adam Smith wrote, "Kindness is the parent of kindness; and if to be beloved by our brethren be the great object of our ambition, the surest way of obtaining it is, by our conduct, to show that we really love them." Other perspectives are social or evolutionary, stressing the advantages to society or the survival advantages of fairness.

---

**Negative Outcomes of Greed:** The idea that greed can backfire to produce negative outcomes is dramatically portrayed in the movie *Wall Street* (1987). In a famous speech, the unethical financier Gekko (played by Michael Douglas) summarizes by saying, "The point, ladies and gentleman, is that greed — for lack of a better word — is good." While the film cannot be shown in many classrooms because of its R rating, Gekko's memorable speech is available online at http://www.americanrhetoric.com/MovieSpeeches/moviespeechwallstreet.html. The speech has become a classic in business communications studies, including one article that provides useful hints on student PowerPoint presentations: Gary H. Jones, "Message First: Using Films to Power the Point," *Business Communication Quarterly* 67, no. 1: 88-91.

**The Cost of Greed:** For further reading, see Sam Pizzigati, *Greed and Good: Understanding and Overcoming the Inequality that Limits Our Lives* (New York: The Apex Press, 2004). This strongly written book carefully examines but rejects "the case for greed" before documenting "the cost of greed." The author concludes by making the case for a "10 times" rule: confiscatory taxation on people who receive more than 10 times a minimum-wage level of income.

**Business and Profits:** See Milton Friedman, "The Social Responsibility of Business Is to Increase its Profits," *The New York Times Magazine*, September 13, 1970. This classic argument for self-interested behavior by corporations does not say that "greed is good" but rather that corporations most effectively serve social responsibility if they seek to "make as much money as possible while conforming to the basic rules of the society, both those embodied in law and those embodied in ethical custom." An abbreviated version of Friedman's article is found in Lesson 9 of this book.

**Motivation:** The John Stossel television program *Greed* (ABC/Disney) has several examples of how self-interest motivates people to serve the interests of others. Each example provides the opportunity for classroom discussion. *Greed* is available from http://www.economicthinking.org/Stossel/index.htm

## VISUAL 2.1
## SELF-INTEREST VS. GREED

In economics, we often assume that people rationally seek their own interests.

But greed, an excessive desire for more money or goods, is not a virtue.

Self-interest can produce good outcomes.

Why do you expect to receive food when you go to a fast-food restaurant?

Writing more than 200 years ago, Adam Smith answered a similar question in the terms of his own time:

> "It is not from the benevolence of the butcher, the brewer, or the baker that we expect our dinner, but from their regard to their own self-interest. We address ourselves, not to their humanity but to their self-love, and never talk to them of our own necessities but of their advantages." (Adam Smith, *The Wealth of Nations*, eds. R.H. Campbell and A.S. Skinner, Indianapolis: Liberty Press, 1981 [1776], 26-27)

How might Adam Smith express this point if he were writing today, using modern sellers as examples?

## VISUAL 2.2
## THE ULTIMATUM GAME: DIRECTIONS

You are about to play a famous game called the Ultimatum Game. In this game players negotiate the division of 10 rewards items. The teacher will define the specific rewards to be allocated. Read these rules, but don't begin to play until your teacher says "Go."

**1.** You play this game in pairs; one player is the Proposer and the other is the Responder.

**2.** If you are the Proposer, your job is to propose an allocation, or division, of 10 rewards items between yourself and a Responder. You may not use fractional amounts, so you must propose a whole number between 0 and 10 rewards for yourself, with the remainder of the 10 rewards going to the Responder.

**3.** If you are the Responder, your job is to accept or reject the Proposer's proposal. If you accept the proposal, both of you will get the proposed number of rewards at the end of the lesson. If you reject the offer, neither of you will get anything for this round.

**4.** Proposers will randomly pick Responders for each round (try not to pick your close friends). Players must switch partners after each round. Do not repeat partners.

**5.** Half the class will start the game as Proposers and half as Responders. You will play two rounds, with a new partner for each round. After the second round, you will switch roles: Each Responder becomes a Proposer, and each Proposer becomes a Responder. You will play two more rounds — again, with a new partner for each round.

**6.** Record your results after each round on the score sheet below. At the end of the game, calculate the total rewards you earned.

**7.** All rewards will be distributed at the end of the lesson.

# VISUAL 2.2 (continued)
# THE ULTIMATUM GAME: DIRECTIONS

| | Proposed division of 10 rewards | | | (P) | (R) |
|---|---|---|---|---|---|
| Round | Number of rewards for **Proposer** | Number of rewards for **Responder** | **Responder's** action | Number of rewards **Proposer** gets | Number of rewards **Responder** gets |
| 1 | | | ☐ Accept ☐ Reject | | |
| 2 | | | ☐ Accept ☐ Reject | | |

*Now switch roles, with Responders becoming Proposers and Proposers becoming Responders.*

| | Proposed division of 10 rewards | | | (P) | (R) |
|---|---|---|---|---|---|
| Round | Number of rewards for **Proposer** | Number of rewards for **Responder** | **Responder's** action | Number of rewards **Proposer** gets | Number of rewards **Responder** gets |
| 3 | | | ☐ Accept ☐ Reject | | |
| 4 | | | ☐ Accept ☐ Reject | | |

**1.** In the column marked (P), circle the number of rewards you earned as a Proposer.
The total number of rewards I get as a Proposer is _____.

**2.** In the column marked (R), circle the number of rewards you earned as a Responder.
The total number of rewards I get as a Responder is _____.

**3.** Add up the total rewards you earned as both a Proposer and Responder.

The total number of rewards I get is _____ .

## VISUAL 2.3
## THE ULTIMATUM GAME: RESULTS

The Ultimatum Game is often played in a controlled setting using computers so that neither the Proposer nor the Responder knows whom they are playing with. In this controlled setting, friendship or calculation of future interaction does not influence behavior.

• In games played multiple times, the average amount offered in a division of $10 is about $2.50.

• By contrast, strict economic logic would say that Proposers should make offers approaching zero and Responders should accept any offer, even one as low as $1.

## Questions

**1.** If you saw $1 lying on the parking lot, would you bend down to pick it up?

**2.** If so, why wouldn't Responders accept an offer of $1 in an Ultimatum Game?

**3.** How do ethical concerns alter the strict economic logic?

For further details, see Richard Thaler, "The Ultimatum Game," *Journal of Economic Perspectives* 2, no. 4 (1988): 195-206.

# ACTIVITY 2.1
# THE ULTIMATUM GAME: DIRECTIONS

You are about to play a famous game called the Ultimatum Game. In this game players negotiate the division of 10 rewards items. The teacher will define the specific rewards to be allocated. Read these rules, but don't begin to play until your teacher says "Go."

**1.** You play this game in pairs; one player is the Proposer and the other is the Responder.

**2.** If you are the Proposer, your job is to propose an allocation, or division, of 10 rewards items between yourself and a Responder. You may not use fractional amounts, so you must propose a whole number between 0 and 10 rewards for yourself, with the remainder of the 10 rewards going to the Responder.

**3.** If you are the Responder, your job is to accept or reject the Proposer's proposal. If you accept the proposal, both of you will get the proposed number of rewards at the end of the lesson. If you reject the offer, neither of you will get anything for this round.

**4.** Proposers will randomly pick Responders for each round (try not to pick your close friends). Players must switch partners after each round. Do not repeat partners.

**5.** Half the class will start the game as Proposers and half as Responders. You will play two rounds, with a new partner for each round. After the second round, you will switch roles: Each Responder becomes a Proposer, and each Proposer becomes a Responder. You will play two more rounds — again, with a new partner for each round.

**6.** Record your results after each round on the score sheet below. At the end of the game, calculate the total rewards you earned.

**7.** All rewards will be distributed at the end of the lesson.

## ACTIVITY 2.1 (continued)
## THE ULTIMATUM GAME: DIRECTIONS

| Round | Proposed division of 10 rewards | | Responder's action | (P) | (R) |
|---|---|---|---|---|---|
| | Number of rewards for **Proposer** | Number of rewards for **Responder** | | Number of rewards **Proposer** gets | Number of rewards **Responder** gets |
| 1 | | | ☐ Accept ☐ Reject | | |
| 2 | | | ☐ Accept ☐ Reject | | |

*Now switch roles, with Responders becoming Proposers and Proposers becoming Responders.*

| Round | Proposed division of 10 rewards | | Responder's action | (P) | (R) |
|---|---|---|---|---|---|
| | Number of rewards for **Proposer** | Number of rewards for **Responder** | | Number of rewards **Proposer** gets | Number of rewards **Responder** gets |
| 3 | | | ☐ Accept ☐ Reject | | |
| 4 | | | ☐ Accept ☐ Reject | | |

**1.** In the column marked (P), circle the number of rewards you earned as a Proposer.

The total number of rewards I get as a Proposer is _____.

**2.** In the column marked (R), circle the number of rewards you earned as a Responder.

The total number of rewards I get as a Responder is _____.

**3.** Add up the total rewards you earned as both a Proposer and Responder.

The total number of rewards I get is _____.

# Lesson 3 – Do Markets Need Ethical Standards?

*The students play the roles of doctors and patients to see how enlightened self-interest, duty and virtue improve economic efficiency.*

## OVERVIEW

### Economics

One of the powerful insights into the economic way of thinking is how people respond to incentives that affect their personal well-being. Consumers and producers each attempt to enhance their own self-interest in purchasing and producing. Yet people's concern for fairness and justice also affects their economic choices, especially in situations that involve fiduciary responsibilities. People who operate from a perspective of duty or character can enhance economic efficiency in markets where asymmetric information and moral hazard exist.

### Ethics

Ethics is the study of right and wrong behavior, or how people think they ought to live. Three main types of ethical systems can guide behavior:

1. Acting to produce outcomes that best satisfy some criterion (for example, human welfare)

2. Acting in a manner consistent with your duty to a rule or principle (for example, the Ten Commandments)

3. Acting from a habit of character consistent with your notion of virtue

Economists are most familiar with the first type of ethical system, which is based on the desirability of producing outcomes consistent with a goal (for example, satisfying consumer preferences). While self-interest is often the dominant motive for many economic actions, considerations of a different nature sometimes play a role in the actions of economic agents in certain market settings. Both duty and character at times provide equally strong rationales for action.

## LESSON DESCRIPTION

The students participate in an exercise that demonstrates the motives of self-interest, duty and character in economic transactions. Playing the roles of doctors and patients, the students experience how asymmetric information can lead to a moral hazard. They experience how differing incentives and moral frameworks can alter the behavior of doctors. Based on the results of the role-play, the students will see how enlightened self-interest, duty and virtue play a role in improving economic efficiency in health-care and other markets.

## CONCEPTS

Asymmetric information
Character
Competition
Duty
Enlightened self-interest
Fiduciary duty
Incentives
Moral hazard
Self-interest

## CONTENT STANDARDS

4. People respond predictably to positive and negative incentives.

9. Competition among sellers lowers costs and prices, and encourages producers to produce more of what consumers are willing and able to buy. Competition among buyers increases prices and allocates goods and services to those people who are willing and able to pay the most for them.

10. Institutions evolve in market economies to help individuals and groups accomplish their goals. Banks, labor unions, corporations, legal systems, and not-for-profit organizations are examples of important institutions. A different kind of institution,

clearly defined and well enforced property rights, is essential to a market economy.

## OBJECTIVES

The students will:

1. Analyze how economic actors at times operate from different ethical perspectives.

2. Participate in an activity that illustrates how different ethical perspectives can produce different economic outcomes.

3. Demonstrate how ethical behavior can enhance economic efficiency when asymmetric information creates a moral hazard.

## TIME REQUIRED

75 minutes

## MATERIALS

1. Visuals 3.1 and 3.2

2. Two copies of Activity 3.1 for two or three class "doctors"

3. Enough copies of Activity 3.2 for the rest of the students in the class to have two Patient Charts
   (**Note:** Before class, make two copies of Activity 3.1 and cut them so you have two instruction sheets for each doctor role. Make enough copies of Activity 3.2 for the rest of the students to have two Patient Charts. Randomly select and record a pain level on each Patient Chart. (The game doesn't require an equal number of pain levels, but make sure all the levels are represented among the patients.) Use one set of doctor instructions and Patient Charts for Round 1 of the game and the second set for Round 2.)

4. One copy of Activity 3.3 for each student

## PROCEDURE

1. Tell the students that they are going to play a game that illustrates how ethical conduct can affect economic efficiency. In health care, for example, consumers do not have the same information as doctors about treatments and costs. Moreover, since insurance pays most of the bills for many people, consumers have little incentive to get more information. The students will see how transparency, *competition*, *incentives* and ethical values affect market outcomes in this situation.

2. Pick three students to play the roles of Doctor A, Doctor B and Doctor C. All other students will play the part of patients. (**Note:** In classes with fewer than 18 students, use only Doctor A and Doctor B.)

3. This step is key. Give each doctor the relevant instructions from Activity 3.1. Separately review with each doctor how you expect him or her to behave, as indicated on the instructions. Tell Doctors A and B that they must follow the very precise instructions they've been given in all cases. Tell Doctor C that he or she has some discretion in each case. Make sure each doctor is clear about the instructions.

4. Choose a student to be record keeper (or do this yourself). Give each of the remaining students a Patient Chart from Activity 3.2 with the pain level already filled in. Tell the patients they have health insurance that will pay 95 percent of the doctors' treatment costs.

5. Position the doctors around the room. Randomly assign patients to the doctors in roughly equal numbers. Doctors will examine the patients' charts and fill in each patient's treatment and cost. The patients then bring their charts to the record keeper, who fills in pain level and cost information on Visual 3.1.
   (**Note:** Do not display Visual 3.1 until the record keeper has filled in all the data.)

6. After all patient data have been recorded, display the completed Visual 3.1. Tell the students that all patients suffered from a backache of varying pain intensity. Review the correct treatments and costs for each pain level as shown on Visual 3.1.

7. Inform the students that "waste" is generated when a market produces something of no value. Use Visual 3.1 to calculate the amount of "waste" for each doctor: the difference between the cost of the treatments the doctor "prescribed" and the cheapest treatment for each pain level. For example, if a patient had a Level 1 pain, the correct treatment was medicine that cost $100. If the doctor charged the patient $500 for an X-ray, this was a waste of $400. Have the record keeper total the amount of waste for each doctor at the bottom of Activity 3.1 and then calculate the total waste for all doctors combined.

8. Ask the students why some doctors had more waste than others. Accept all answers, and write them on the board or on a transparency. This sets the stage for the discussion that follows.

9. Now tell the students that all the doctors had the same training and experience and they were not concerned about malpractice lawsuits. Ask the students playing doctors to state the goal they were instructed to achieve in treating their patients. Make sure the students understand that each doctor had different instructions, and ask them if they think the instructions had any impact on each doctor's waste. Doctor A was instructed not to consider profit in deciding which treatment to choose and to charge only for the correct treatment, so Doctor A had no incentive to prescribe more-expensive treatments that would create waste. Doctor B was instructed to maximize short-run profit and prescribe a more-expensive treatment for all patients, which created waste. Doctor C was instructed to maximize long-run profits and could choose any treatment for each

patient. If Doctor C isn't greedy, this doctor would likely prescribe the appropriate treatment for most patients, creating little waste.

10. Ask the following questions to lead a class discussion about the characteristics of this particular market that enabled some doctors to overcharge.

A. Compared with doctors, how much do patients know about the correct treatment for backache? *Often very little. Studying medicine requires eight or more years of education and training beyond the high school level. Thus, there is a market condition of asymmetric information.*

B. How hard is it for patients to get better information? What search costs are involved? *Patients can read books, search the Internet and talk to other patients. They can seek a second opinion from another doctor. However, if patients are in great pain or have a life-threatening injury, they will likely want immediate treatment from the first provider they see, and searching is very costly in terms of time and money. Sometimes a major cost to patients is the opportunity cost of taking time off from work to visit alternative doctors. Some medical plans make it difficult to get a second opinion because patients must go through a primary-care provider. In a small town there may not be competing doctors. Some patients may also feel embarrassed about getting a second opinion, as this may suggest a lack of confidence in their primary doctor.*

C. What economic incentive do patients have to get good pricing information in this market? *The economic incentives will be weak as long as insurance companies pay most of the expenses. To some extent, patients understand that insurance premiums will rise as these expenses increase. But this understanding probably won't have much effect on patients unless they feel some sense of ethical responsibility about not overusing medical resources.*

**D.** How transparent are the transactions in a doctor's office, in terms of treatments ordered and prices charged? *By "transparent" we mean that consumers can readily see what other patients are paying for similar services. Medical treatments are usually not publicly known because of patient confidentiality. Since third parties (insurance companies) usually pay a large percentage of health-care bills, patients are often unaware of the total cost of their own treatments. The Internet, however, provides an excellent way for patients to more easily find and communicate with each other about medical providers.*

**E.** What different motives might different doctors bring to these transactions? *Many doctors adhere to the Hippocratic Oath (Activity 3.3) because they believe it is part of their duty to put the patients' interests first. Other doctors might be motivated by greed, focusing on personal, short-run profit and ignoring their moral obligations to others. Other doctors might follow enlightened self-interest, which is to behave honestly so they can attract more clients in the long run. Other doctors behave honestly because they genuinely desire to have this virtuous character trait.*

11. Play the second round of the game. Select two or three new doctors, based on the size of the class. On Visual 3.2, label each new doctor by the student's name, for example, "Doctor Mary" and "Doctor Joe." Give each new doctor a set of instructions from Activity 3.1. Do not let patients know who is assigned the roles of Doctors A, B and C. Position the doctors in different areas of the room.

12. Give each patient a new chart with the pain level already filled in. This time tell the

patients that they and not their insurance company will be responsible for paying all treatment expenses. Tell them that after their treatment, they will give their chart to the record keeper, who will immediately post the cost information on Visual 3.2.

13. Start by having only one patient visit each doctor. (If there are three doctors, there should be only three patients.) Immediately record the pain level and the cost each doctor charges his or her patient on Visual 3.2.

14. Allow the other patients to select the doctor they want to visit. Reinforce the idea that patients now pay the full cost. The goal is for patients to use the information on Visual 3.2 to help them pick a doctor. (**Note:** If the class is small, you can give each patient two Patient Charts to get more information.)

15. After all the patients have turned in their charts, ask the record keeper to total the waste for each doctor and then for all the doctors combined. Ask the students to explain why the total waste for all the doctors is less in this round. *It is likely that patients will gravitate toward doctors who provide the correct treatment at the lowest cost for their pain level. Bring out these key points:*
    - *Consumers who pay their own bills have an economic incentive to search for better service at lower prices.*
    - *Competition acts as a powerful force to make sellers behave honestly as long as no collusion is possible.*
    - *For competition to work best, market transactions must be transparent or the market must have some way of transmitting honest intent such as providing extended warranties.*
    - *When transparency does not exist, or when third parties such as insurance companies pay the bills, ethical conduct or enlightened self-interest is needed to promote greater economic efficiency.*

16. Distribute a copy of Activity 3.3 to each student. Allow a few minutes for reading. Discuss the answers to the questions.

**Question 1.** Define these terms: asymmetric information, moral hazard and fiduciary relationship. *Asymmetric information exists when one party to a transaction has better information than another party and it is expensive or impossible for the less-knowledgeable party to get this information.*

*Moral hazard arises when an economic agent has an economic incentive to behave unethically. For example, a doctor has both the ability and an economic incentive to impose higher costs on health insurance companies for personal gain.*

*A fiduciary relationship arises when one party to a transaction is a dominant party and the other is vulnerable because of confidential information or other disparity. The dominant actor is entrusted with fiduciary power over a weak party in return for considerations of fairness and trust.*

**Question 2.** Give examples of situations in which people expect fiduciary conduct. *Answers will vary and include a lawyer and a client, a priest and a confessor, a teacher and a student, a psychologist and a patient, an engineer and a construction company, a certified public accountant and the public, a chairman of a company and the company's shareholders.*

**Question 3.** What motivates many professionals to adhere to fiduciary rules of conduct in serving their clients?

*Duty: They adhere to the intellectual principle that it is their obligation to put their clients' interests first.*

*Outcomes: They have an enlightened self-interest and know that if they treat clients well, they will attract more customers and profits in the long run. Also, by adhering to fiduciary standards, they do not need to worry about the penalties of getting caught for fraud.*

*Virtuous Character: Many people like to see themselves as honest and upright. They would not enjoy the extra money they earned if it came from taking unfair advantage of people who are in weak or vulnerable positions.*

**Question 4.** Which do you think best promotes honest behavior and economic efficiency: government regulations and penalties, enlightened self-interest in markets or ethical character? *People respond predictably to negative incentives such as harsher government penalties for getting convicted and stronger regulations for monitoring business fraud; so, stronger regulations could promote more honest behavior. However, this is a costly way to achieve the objective. There are explicit and implicit costs associated with government regulations. Explicit costs include hiring staff (police, prosecutors, judges and jail keepers) and increasing taxes to pay for the new employees. Companies also incur explicit business expenses to comply with rules and regulations (hiring extra staff to monitor and fill out reports). Implicit costs to society include the loss of business freedom and the potential for corruption of government officials. Hence, while it is possible to rely on negative incentives to promote ethical behavior, it is expensive to do so.*

*By contrast, relying upon enlightened self-interest and ethical character enhances both efficiency and freedom. Competition rewards providers who behave honestly. In markets that lack transparency, however, even enlightened self-interest may fail to promote honesty. This is because a greedy person is always calculating whether it is profitable to be honest, and changing circumstances could change behavior. A person of ethical character is always honest, because this is the right thing to do.*

## CLOSURE

17. Ask the students to review the types of market situations in which fiduciary duty arises. *Fiduciary duty arises in situations where asymmetric information and moral-hazard problems exist and there is a strong need for public trust.*

18. Review the characteristics of fiduciary duty. *Fiduciary duty involves a confidence or trust. It arises when a dominant party has power over a weak or vulnerable party. For more than 2,000 years doctors have taken the Hippocratic or a similar oath, which obliges them to put their patients' interests ahead of the profit motive. Accountants, lawyers, teachers, engineers, journalists, priests and many other professionals, in theory, maintain an allegiance first to their profession and its fiduciary standards and second to the specific organization for which they work. Chief executive officers of companies must also demonstrate fiduciary conduct by putting the interests of shareholders ahead of their own interests.*

**The bottom line:** Ethical standards create the institutional framework within which businesses operate. Trust generated by ethical conduct enhances economic efficiency by reducing transaction costs and waste.

## ASSESSMENT

### Multiple-Choice Questions

3.1 Markets are more efficient when the following characteristics are present:
   A. Economic actors are self-interested.
   B. Market activities are transparent.
   C. Economic actors uphold ethical standards of behavior.
   **D. All of the above**

3.2 A company board of directors hires a chief financial officer to carry out activities on behalf of the stockholders. This situation reflects
   A. a corporate hazard.
   **B. fiduciary duty.**
   C. ideology.
   D. none of the above.

3.3 Frank learns that an inherited genetic disease affects people in his family. This disease will likely cause early death. Frank immediately applies for a large life-insurance policy without disclosing this genetic fact. This situation
   A. is economically efficient because Frank gets to buy the insurance he wants.
   B. is economically efficient because Frank's family will need the money when he dies.
   **C. is economically inefficient because of asymmetric information.**
   D. is economically inefficient because of a fiduciary relationship.

### Essay Questions

3.1 Analyze the extent and impact of fiduciary conduct in the operation of business. *Fiduciary conduct greatly aids the efficiency of all organizations, including for-profit businesses. Fiduciary conduct is an integral part of the work done by accountants, lawyers, financial officers and company chief executives. It is also an integral part of the expectations of company managers and workers at every level. Every worker holds a fiduciary trust.*

**3.2** Analyze how transparency affects the efficiency of markets. In markets that lack transparency, what role does ethical conduct play? *Transparency is a key tool to making markets work efficiently for consumers and producers. If some prices are not disclosed openly (as in health care), then it is harder for consumers to protect themselves. In such cases, ethical conduct is required — hence, virtually every professional society maintains an ethical code of conduct (see Going Further).*

## GOING FURTHER

**Doctors and Profits:** Some doctors earn higher profits when they order expensive lab tests and imaging procedures for patients. While such kickbacks are illegal, they are hard to discover, and there are also technical maneuvers around the laws. See David Armstrong, "MRI and CT Centers Offer Doctors Way to Profit on Scans," *The Wall Street Journal*, May 2, 2005, A1.

**Doctors and Asymmetric Information:** 1972 Nobel Prize winner Kenneth Arrow discussed the problem of doctors, asymmetric information and ethics in *The Limits of Organization* (New York: Norton, 1974). For an example of poor information leading to abuse, see Paul Davies, "Flawed Procedures: A Doctor's Tale Shows Weakness in Medical Vetting," *The Wall Street Journal*, September 21, 2005, A1.

**Professional Codes of Ethics:** Many professions have ethical codes of conduct. The students can do an Internet search for the phrase "code of ethics" to see the wide range of professions covered, from realtors to bankers to social workers.

**Nobel Prize Winners:** In 2001 George A. Ackerlof, A. Michael Spence and Joseph E. Stiglitz received the Nobel Prize in Economics for their work analyzing markets with asymmetric information. For further reading, see http://nobelprize.org/economics/laureates/2001/press.html

**Market Responses to Information Problems**: Ask the students how markets might respond when there is a desire for more information in a transaction. For example:

• When people apply for life insurance, what health tests must they take? Why is this information necessary for proper pricing in life-insurance markets?

• When someone sells a used car, how does the offer of a free warranty provide information to consumers? How does a free warranty affect market demand?

• If you are traveling through a new town and want to buy a hamburger, how do you know where to go? How does a franchise such as McDonald's or Burger King provide information about quality?

# VISUAL 3.1
# PAIN, COST AND WASTE (ROUND 1)

| Pain Level | Correct Treatment | Cost |
|---|---|---|
| 1 | Medicine | $ 100 |
| 2 | X-Ray | $ 500 |
| 3 | Surgery | $2,000 |

| Patient | Doctor A | | | Doctor B | | | Doctor C | | |
|---|---|---|---|---|---|---|---|---|---|
| | Pain Level | Cost | Waste | Pain Level | Cost | Waste | Pain Level | Cost | Waste |
| 1 | | | | | | | | | |
| 2 | | | | | | | | | |
| 3 | | | | | | | | | |
| 4 | | | | | | | | | |
| 5 | | | | | | | | | |
| 6 | | | | | | | | | |
| 7 | | | | | | | | | |
| 8 | | | | | | | | | |
| 9 | | | | | | | | | |
| 10 | | | | | | | | | |
| 11 | | | | | | | | | |
| 12 | | | | | | | | | |
| 13 | | | | | | | | | |
| 14 | | | | | | | | | |
| 15 | | | | | | | | | |

| Total Waste | Doctor A | | Doctor B | | Doctor C | |
|---|---|---|---|---|---|---|

**Total Waste All Doctors**

# VISUAL 3.2
# PAIN, COST AND WASTE (ROUND 2)

| Pain Level | Correct Treatment | Cost |
|---|---|---|
| 1 | Medicine | $ 100 |
| 2 | X-Ray | $ 500 |
| 3 | Surgery | $2,000 |

| Patient | Doctor: Pain Level | Cost | Waste | Doctor: Pain Level | Cost | Waste | Doctor: Pain Level | Cost | Waste |
|---|---|---|---|---|---|---|---|---|---|
| 1 | | | | | | | | | |
| 2 | | | | | | | | | |
| 3 | | | | | | | | | |
| 4 | | | | | | | | | |
| 5 | | | | | | | | | |
| 6 | | | | | | | | | |
| 7 | | | | | | | | | |
| 8 | | | | | | | | | |
| 9 | | | | | | | | | |
| 10 | | | | | | | | | |
| 11 | | | | | | | | | |
| 12 | | | | | | | | | |
| 13 | | | | | | | | | |
| 14 | | | | | | | | | |
| 15 | | | | | | | | | |

Total Waste Doctor: ___   Doctor: ___   Doctor: ___

**Total Waste All Doctors** ___

# ACTIVITY 3.1
# INSTRUCTIONS FOR DOCTORS

## INSTRUCTIONS FOR DOCTOR A

**1.** There are three possible treatments for a BACKACHE. The chart below shows the "correct" treatment for each pain level. The profit you earn is directly proportional to the patient's cost. You do not need to worry about any of your patients suing you for malpractice.

| Pain Level | Correct Treatment | Cost |
|---|---|---|
| 1 | Medicine | $ 100 |
| 2 | X-Ray | $ 500 |
| 3 | Surgery | $2,000 |

**2.** Important! You must NOT consider your own profit in deciding which treatment to choose. Charge only for the correct treatment based on each patient's level of pain.
**Example:** Give a patient with Level 2 pain an X-ray and charge $500.

**3.** Record your treatment and cost on each patient's chart, circle your name and give the chart back to the patient.

## INSTRUCTIONS FOR DOCTOR B

**1.** There are three possible treatments for a BACKACHE. The chart below shows the "correct" treatment for each pain level. The profit you earn is directly proportional to the patient's cost. You do not need to worry about any of your patients suing you for malpractice.

| Pain Level | Correct Treatment | Cost |
|---|---|---|
| 1 | Medicine | $ 100 |
| 2 | X-Ray | $ 500 |
| 3 | Surgery | $2,000 |

**2.** Important! Your goal is to maximize your short-run profit. To do this, charge ALL patients for treatment at the next higher level of pain.
**Examples:** Give a patient with Level 1 pain the Level 2 treatment: an X-ray costing $500. Give a patient with Level 2 pain Level 3 treatment: surgery costing $2,000.

**3.** Record your treatment and cost on each patient's chart, circle your name and give the chart back to the patient.

# ACTIVITY 3.1 (continued)
# INSTRUCTIONS FOR DOCTORS

**INSTRUCTIONS FOR DOCTOR C**

**1.** There are three possible treatments for a BACKACHE. The chart below shows the minimum treatment cost, based on pain level. The profit you earn is directly proportional to the patient's cost. You do not need to worry about any of your patients suing you for malpractice.

| Pain Level | Correct Treatment | Minimum Cost |
|---|---|---|
| 1 | Medicine | $ 100 |
| 2 | X-Ray | $ 500 |
| 3 | Surgery | $2,000 |

**2.** Important! Your goal is to maximize your long-run profit over many years. You can earn higher profits in the short run by charging a higher price than the minimums shown above.
**Example:** You could give a patient with Level 1 pain a medicine but charge $200; or you could give this patient Level 2 treatment, an X-ray, and charge $500.
Balance your desire for higher profits today with your desire to keep patients coming back to you in the future. Charge accordingly.

**3.** Record your treatment and cost on each patient's chart, circle your name and give the chart back to the patient.

# ACTIVITY 3.2
# PATIENT SYMPTOMS

---

**PATIENT CHART**

**1.** Patients: You are suffering from a BACKACHE with the pain level shown below.
Present this chart to a doctor for treatment.

Pain level:                    (Low)    1    2    3    (High)

**2.** Doctor:    **A.** Circle ONE Treatment:    Medicine    X-ray    Surgery

**B.** Cost:    _____

**C.** Circle your name:    Dr. A    Dr. B    Dr. C

**3.** Patients: After visiting the doctor, please turn this sheet in to the record keeper.

---

**PATIENT CHART**

**1.** Patients: You are suffering from a BACKACHE with the pain level shown below.
Present this chart to a doctor for treatment.

Pain level:                    (Low)    1    2    3    (High)

**2.** Doctor:    **A.** Circle ONE Treatment:    Medicine    X-ray    Surgery

**B.** Cost:    _____

**C.** Circle your name:    Dr. A    Dr. B    Dr. C

**3.** Patients: After visiting the doctor, please turn this sheet in to the record keeper.

---

**PATIENT CHART**

**1.** Patients: You are suffering from a BACKACHE with the pain level shown below.
Present this chart to a doctor for treatment.

Pain level:                    (Low)    1    2    3    (High)

**2.** Doctor:    **A.** Circle ONE Treatment:    Medicine    X-ray    Surgery

**B.** Cost:    _____

**C.** Circle your name:    Dr. A    Dr. B    Dr. C

**3.** Patients: After visiting the doctor, please turn this sheet in to the record keeper.

---

# ACTIVITY 3.3
# ASYMMETRIC INFORMATION AND MORAL HAZARD

**Directions:** Read this information and be prepared to discuss the answers to the questions in class.

Sanjay goes to a doctor because of a severe and sudden backache. Brenda's car breaks down on the highway and is towed to the nearest garage. What is similar about these situations? In both cases, the consumers have much less information about the costs and benefits of the proposed service than the sellers. Both situations are examples of *asymmetric information.*[1]

Sanjay's and Brenda's problems are potentially serious. The doctor and the mechanic can recommend very expensive procedures that provide no value. For example, the mechanic could replace the transmission when the old one only needed oil. This is pure waste to the consumer, and learning from this incident is not very helpful when it comes to future car trouble because transmissions are very different from, say, mufflers. More importantly, Sanjay and Brenda are presenting themselves to doctors and mechanics at a time of emergency. It may not be possible for a patient to seek a second opinion or for a stranded motorist to shop around for a garage. Customers may also be distraught and unable to think rationally.

Asymmetric information produces a *moral hazard* in which the doctor or the mechanic has an economic incentive to behave unethically by imposing higher costs on Sanjay or Brenda. One moral claim is to maximize company profits by charging the most the market will bear; the other moral claim is to treat Sanjay and Brenda fairly. Asymmetric information makes it difficult for consumers (and sometimes producers) to protect themselves. Some consumers also cannot be expected to make informed choices because of age or mental capacity. Ethical behavior is often expected in society when the potential for a moral hazard exists; think about the rules of behavior for judges, priests and teachers. *Fiduciary duty* thus relates to, or involves, a confidence or trust. A fiduciary trust arises when a dominant party is entrusted with power over a weak or vulnerable party. Most professional societies maintain ethical codes of conduct that address fiduciary duties.

Problems of asymmetric information are often handled adequately by *enlightened self-interest* in the marketplace. Consumers, for example, have an ethical duty to use reasonable diligence in selecting products and providers. The phrase *caveat emptor* captures this idea: Let the buyer beware. In addition, the mechanic at the car-repair shop may not seek to take advantage of Brenda's vulnerability, hoping to earn a reputation for honesty. Repeat business is a powerful reason to put consumers' interests first.

## ACTIVITY 3.3 (continued)
## ASYMMETRIC INFORMATION AND MORAL HAZARD

But in some settings it is not enough to rely upon enlightened self-interest or consumer vigilance alone. Unbridled greed can lead to problems of inefficiency. Society seeks to minimize opportunistic greed through the use of *incentives*. Positive incentives arise through socialization and the rewards for good conduct. Doing the "right" thing for the sake of doing the right thing — and not for a cost/benefit calculation — is the foundation of many ethical systems today (Kantian, Christian, Jewish and Islamic codes).

Negative incentives hold unethical behaviors in check through fear of public exposure and through judicial penalties for fraud. However, it is expensive for government to monitor markets, and even more expensive to prosecute people and companies that engage in deception. Government regulations act as a "tax" on all businesses, even those that are honest. Moreover, the existence of "Big Brother" may create a sense of paternalism, which reduces the public's own watchfulness. Hence, relying mainly upon negative incentives in the form of regulations and penalties is an expensive way to deal with moral hazards. There are not enough police or judges to promote honest behavior unless most citizens desire honesty. If internal self-command exists, government resources can be focused on the "outlier" bad cases.

Hippocrates (460 to 377 B.C.) outlined the moral rule for physicians that stresses their duty to act in the interests of patients and disregard their own private gain. While many of Hippocrates' specific rules are considered outdated by modern practitioners, the concept of requiring an ethical code for doctors is accepted today in virtually every medical school. "I will keep [my patients] from harm and injustice . . . . In purity and holiness I will guard my life and my art." [2]

Image: Courtesy of the National Library of Medicine

---

[1] Some differences in information are trivial. For example, a maker of aspirin stuffs a large bottle with cotton, and the buyers gets fewer pills than anticipated. This merits little attention because the stakes are low, and consumers can easily adjust their behavior in the future without much cost. It is also important to note that in some cases buyers have better information than sellers, for example, in the market for life insurance.

[2] From Ludwig Edelstein, *The Hippocratic Oath: Text, Translation, and Interpretation* (Baltimore: Johns Hopkins Press, 1943). Translation from the Greek by Ludwig Edelstein. Source: http://www.pbs.org/wgbh/nova/doctors/oath_classical.html

# ACTIVITY 3.3 (continued)
# ASYMMETRIC INFORMATION AND MORAL HAZARD

## Questions

**1.** Define these terms: asymmetric information, moral hazard and fiduciary relationship.

**2.** Give examples of situations in which people expect fiduciary conduct.

**3.** What motivates many professionals to adhere to fiduciary rules of conduct in serving their clients?

**4.** Which do you think best promotes honest behavior and economic efficiency: government regulations and penalties, enlightened self-interest in markets or ethical character?

# Lesson 4 — Do Markets Make Us More Moral?

*The students apply economic analysis to a case study of discrimination to demonstrate how market incentives can reward the development of virtuous character traits such as hard work, honesty and acceptance of others.*

## OVERVIEW

### Economics

Behavior in the private sector is sometimes associated with questionable moral practices, as in the high-profile scandals involving Enron Corporation and Global Crossing, for example. Adam Smith, however, pointed out that competitive markets, in which people seek their own self-interest, can produce good social outcomes. This is true especially compared with alternative systems that rely on coercion or force. Within a supportive institutional framework, modern markets rely on voluntary relationships, respect for private property and promotion of individual freedom. As a result, competitive markets foster certain positive values and behaviors.

### Ethics

The idea that competitive markets might foster morally positive values and behaviors is controversial. Markets have often been associated with a long list of horrors including unbridled greed and evil institutions such as slavery. A closer examination, however, reveals that the absence of markets is often associated with worse moral outcomes. Most people who lived under Marxist rule in China and the former Soviet Union have abandoned the romance and mythology that nonmarket systems still hold for some. Within a supportive system of justice, competitive markets more easily align people's personal interests with society's interests by providing a system of incentives that encourage self-discipline, honesty, tolerance, cooperation, courtesy, enterprise and responsibility.

## LESSON DESCRIPTION

In this lesson the students discuss situations that demonstrate how markets reward moral behavior. Then they apply an economic analysis to discrimination on the basis of race, gender and religion. In doing so, they discuss how people in markets and people in government face different incentives regarding discrimination. Next, they read about and discuss several values that market systems encourage and nonmarket systems discourage. The students also learn that markets do not always function perfectly and aren't capable of handling all of our moral problems; other institutions play important roles in shaping moral values.

## CONCEPTS

Accountability
Cooperation
Courtesy
Discipline
Discrimination
Enterprise
Honesty
Incentives
Invisible hand
Market
Responsibility
Self-interest
Tolerance

## CONTENT STANDARDS

4. People respond predictably to positive and negative incentives.

10. Institutions evolve in market economies to help individuals and groups accomplish their goals. Banks, labor unions, corporations, legal systems, and not-for-profit organizations are examples of important institutions. A different kind of institution, clearly defined and well-enforced property rights, is essential to a market economy.

## OBJECTIVES

The students will:

1. Identify how markets provide incentives to reward several positive values and behaviors.

2. Explain how discrimination on the basis of race, gender and religion can adversely affect revenue and profits.

3. Identify several values and behaviors that markets foster.

4. Identify limitations of markets in fostering positive values.

## TIME REQUIRED

45 minutes

## MATERIALS

1. Visuals 4.1, 4.2, 4.3, 4.4 and 4.5

2. One copy of Activity 4.1 for each student

## PROCEDURE

1. Display only Part A of Visual 4.1. Explain that behavior in the private sector is sometimes associated with questionable moral practices. Discuss how high-profile cases such as Enron and Global Crossing seem to draw our attention.

2. Display the question in Part B of Visual 4.1. Ask the students whether corrupt behavior is a problem that people exhibit only in the private sector. Allow them a chance to respond with examples from their community, then show the answer in Part C of Visual 4.1. Say that people in government and in the nonprofit sector can also behave immorally. Emphasize that immorality exists in all walks of life. Fortunately in the United States, such cases are the exception; thus they command front-page headlines. The United States is a country with generally strong moral behavior, which contributes to our economic success and general well-being.

3. Display Part A of Visual 4.2. Tell the class that people often complain about the selfish behavior they observe in others. They point to high prices of prescription drugs or gasoline as examples and claim that *markets* are the source of these and other problems. They view market systems as fostering unseemly values such as egoism, greed and a winner-take-all attitude.

4. Display the question in Part B of Visual 4.2. Allow the students a chance to respond. You might prod them by asking if they get benefits from watching movies or listening to CDs produced by private companies. You could also ask
   • if they traveled to school in a car or a bus manufactured by a private company.
   • if they enjoy a food produced by a private company.
   • why they tend to buy private-market products rather than a government-produced CD, car or food item. ***Where available, consumer products made by government-owned industries are often an inferior quality and cost more — as anyone who visited the Soviet Union under communism can testify.***

5. After the students have finished responding to these questions, display the answer in Part C of Visual 4.2. Explain that economists focus on how incentives affect behavior. In particular, economists observe that competitive markets provide positive incentives that reward values including respect for others, individual freedom and voluntary *cooperation*. Tell the students that the purpose of this lesson is to examine how market systems may contribute to the formation of positive moral values and behaviors. The lesson also notes that markets are not capable of handling all our moral problems.

   The quote from Adam Smith, the founder of economics, shows how the operation of competitive markets — people seeking their own *self-interest* — often results in good social outcomes. Smith used the term *invisible hand* to describe how people can do good for others by helping themselves. You might point out, for example, that when a business such as Apple Computer Inc. expands its business by offering a new product such as the iPod, it intends primarily to help itself and its shareholders by earning increased revenue and profits. At the same time, however, the new product also benefits others. New jobs are created in the computer and music industries. Consumers have a new product and more music for their personal enjoyment.

6.  Display Part A of Visual 4.3. Go over the scenario with the students.

7.  Display the question in Part B of Visual 4.3. Ask the students which job candidate they would hire and why. Allow them a chance to respond, then show the answer in Part C of Visual 4.3. Explain how the desire to earn a profit provides an incentive for business owners to hire the most productive workers rather than allow prejudice and bias to influence their hiring decisions. Tell the students that discriminatory practices can be unprofitable business practices.

8.  Display Part D of Visual 4.3. Tell the students to note that government hiring, in contrast to hiring in the private sector, involves no consideration of profit, so government may hire workers who have better connections instead of workers who are more productive. This reminds us that other institutions in society can exhibit problems of *discrimination* and immorality, but these institutions may have fewer and weaker mechanisms for enforcing accountability than do businesses.

9.  Display Visual 4.4. Explain that Southern streetcar owners early in the 20th century resisted Jim Crow laws (laws that enforced segregation by race). The streetcar owners may have been as racially biased and prejudiced as other people at the time, but the profit motive influenced them to avoid discriminating against

African Americans because they recognized that nondiscrimination was a wise business decision. The profit motive influenced their desire to resist segregation.

10.  Display Visual 4.5. Explain that competitive markets, while providing powerful economic incentives, are not the only influence on people's behavior. Social norms also influence people's decisions: There was a time, for example, when baseball club owners feared that they would lose revenue from white customers if they did not discriminate. Families, religions, schools and voluntary organizations also affect moral behavior.

11.  Distribute a copy of Activity 4.1 to each student. This activity compares and contrasts the values that market systems promote with the values promoted by nonmarket systems. Have the students read the activity and then briefly discuss the main points as a class. Focus on the reasons why markets work better than command systems and why the values that markets foster are more positive than the values fostered by command systems. Here are some key discussion points:
    •  Markets rely on voluntary relationships rather than force.
    •  Markets create incentives for people to serve others in order to benefit themselves. These incentives operate to keep business interests aligned with society's interests and foster honesty, integrity, hard work and respect for others.
    •  Markets promote individual respect and freedom because the choices of consumers and producers are the basis for exchange.
    •  Markets are more accountable than command systems because profits and prices make information more transparent.
    •  Markets promote respect for private property because property rights are protected.

12.  Ask the students to write the answers to the questions at the end of the reading.

When they have finished the assignment, discuss the answers as a class.

**Question 1.** According to this reading, what is the first economic freedom in a modern market system? *Own yourself*

**Question 2.** Slavery is often regarded as a market institution. After all, it involved many of the characteristics of a market including ownership, prices and exchanges. Do you agree that slavery was a market institution? Explain your answer. *Slavery was not a modern market institution. It depended on involuntary trade. African Americans were forced to provide their labor and were therefore exploited. A free society depends on a system of justice to define and defend property rights. The right to own oneself is a basic property right upheld today by ethical principles and enforced by our legal system (the 13th Amendment to the U.S. Constitution outlawed slavery). A competitive market system relies on voluntary exchanges, not force. This is why Adam Smith called slavery "the unfortunate law," which, he noted, held back progress.*

**Question 3.** How might owning and operating a restaurant encourage values such as honesty, enterprise and courtesy? *If a restaurant owner is dishonest — charging arbitrary prices, serving subprime meats when the menu describes prime cuts, consistently giving incorrect change — customers will not return. Profits will decline. Profits will also decline if the owner is rude to or annoys customers. Few customers want to dine in a restaurant where they are not treated with respect. Enterprising restaurant owners might create new menu items, vary portion sizes to fit the interests of customers or experiment with discounts for families or senior citizens. These owners will likely be rewarded with steady business and healthy profits.*

**Question 4.** How might owning and operating a shoe store encourage values such as tolerance and responsibility? *A profit-motivated shoe-store owner would want to earn the business of all types of people and would not want to discriminate against customers on the basis of race, gender or religion. The desire to earn a profit provides an incentive to tolerate differences in others. Business ownership also encourages responsibility. Losing profits and facing possible bankruptcy are sobering for business owners. They have an incentive to make careful and responsible decisions.*

**Question 5.** How does the construction of a new home encourage cooperation among strangers? *Building a home is a complicated process that depends on many people, usually strangers, to work together. It involves gaining the voluntary cooperation of plumbers, electricians, drywall hangers, painters, carpenters and others. The one thing that makes all these people cooperate with each other is their desire to earn an income.*

13. Explain to the class that markets are limited in their ability to foster positive values and behaviors. It is impossible to know the extent to which competitive markets encourage values such as tolerance and courtesy, as well as the extent to which markets depend on pre-existing values and behaviors. Although competitive markets foster and reinforce certain values and behaviors, markets alone cannot instill them completely. Moral education needs to be the responsibility of other institutions such as families, religious institutions and volunteer organizations.

## CLOSURE

14. Review the main points of the lesson by asking the following questions:

    **A.** Why is it often in the best interest of a business owner not to discriminate on the basis of race, gender or religion? *Businesses pay a penalty for discrimi-*

*nation on the basis of race, gender and religion. Failure to hire the most productive workers or sell to certain customers because of bias or prejudice reduces the owner's chances of increasing revenue and earning a profit.*

**B.** What are some of the values that market systems foster? *Discipline, honesty, tolerance, cooperation, courtesy, enterprise and responsibility*

**C.** What role does a system of justice play in market systems? *A system of justice provides the "rules of the economic game." Specifically, it defines the types and scope of property rights and enforces these rights.*

**The bottom line:** Markets make us more moral: They create incentives for people to serve others in order to benefit themselves. However, moral behavior depends on more than markets and is influenced by institutions such as families, religions, schools and volunteer organizations.

## ASSESSMENT

**Multiple-Choice Questions**

**4.1** Competitive markets promote all of the following behaviors except

A. tolerating the values and opinions of customers.

*B. using force to achieve economic progress.*

C. providing incentives for individuals to serve other people.

D. encouraging individuals to discipline themselves.

**4.2** Even if no laws require it, business owners have an economic incentive to be tolerant when they hire employees and serve customers because of

A. their religious views.

B. their fear of major lawsuits.

C. the Occupational Safety and Health Administration.

*D. the profit motive.*

**4.3** In *The Wealth of Nations*, economist Adam Smith argued that people can help others by helping themselves. His term for this idea was

A. the social-service paradox.

B. benevolent dictator.

*C. the invisible hand.*

D. enlightened self-absorption.

**Essay Questions**

**4.1** In the early 1940s, professional baseball, like much of American society, was characterized by rigid racial segregation. Several baseball club owners were convinced that African-Americans should not play in the major leagues. But in 1947 club owner Branch Rickey brought Jackie Robinson up from the minor leagues to play for the Brooklyn Dodgers. A few years later many African-American players joined major league teams. Why do you suppose Branch Rickey took the risk to sign Jackie Robinson? *He faced incentives to find the most productive players he could. Rickey wanted new talent to help the team win a championship. He hoped a winning team would put more paying customers in the stands, thus enhancing the club's revenue and profits. He sensed that fans would want to watch good baseball regardless of the race of the players. He was willing to risk violating racial codes and put an end to racial discrimination in baseball to be a business success. From the perspective of virtue and character ethics, Rickey may have also acted the way he did because he felt it was the morally right thing to do.*

**4.2** You are the manager of a new boutique coffee shop and art gallery called Frame of Mind. Your immediate task is to complete the training of your three new employees. You have already shown them how to prepare the different coffee drinks, and you have helped them become familiar with the artwork in the gallery and the artists whose work is on display. Now you need to train the employees on the importance of good customer service. Identify and explain two values that you will stress to ensure good customer service and foster positive behavior on the part of your employees. *Answers will vary and may include honesty, tolerance and courtesy. If customers suspect that they are being cheated, they are not likely to return. The store welcomes customers of all races and creeds because all paying customers help employees to earn an income and the shop to earn a profit. Courtesy relates to that old adage in business, "the customer is always right." There are plenty of other coffee shops and art galleries; customers could go to these competitors. Customers are not likely to return to a shop where the staff is rude or disrespectful.*

## GOING FURTHER

**Economics of Discrimination:** Thomas Sowell has written extensively about issues related to racial discrimination. His book *Applied Economics: Thinking Beyond Stage One* (New York: Basic Books, 2004) has a highly accessible chapter titled "The Economics of Discrimination." It provides an insightful analysis of how markets provide incentives that discourage racial and religious discrimination. He cites several examples from different periods in U.S. and world history. This book also contains chapters on the economics of housing and medical care and the economic development of nations.

**Bourgeois Virtue:** Deirdre McCloskey has influenced thinking in the area of values and economics. In "Bourgeois Virtue," (*The American Scholar*, Spring 1994, 177-191), she draws distinctions between three types of virtues — aristocrat, peasant and bourgeois — and explains and defends the virtues of the bourgeoisie (rising middle-class traders and shopkeepers). "The growth of the market, I would argue, promotes virtue, not vice," she writes. "Most intellectuals since 1848 have thought the opposite: that it erodes virtue

. . . . And yet we all take happily what the market gives — polite, accommodating, energetic, enterprising, risk-taking, trustworthy people; not bad people. In the Bulgaria of old . . . the department stores had a policeman on every floor, not to prevent theft but to stop the customers from attacking the arrogant and incompetent clerks selling goods that fell apart at the moment of sale. The way a salesperson in an American store greets customers startles foreigners: 'How can I help you?' It is an instance of miniature bourgeois virtue" (181).

McCloskey elaborates on this theme in *The Bourgeois Virtues* (Chicago: University of Chicago Press, 2006). In this book, she argues that private property, free labor and prudent calculation form the foundation of ethical good in modern society and are not a moral threat to society. She argues that by following antibourgeois values of the proletariat and the aristocracy, "the 20th century paid a butcher's bill."

# VISUAL 4.1
# SELF-INTEREST VS. SOCIAL GOOD

## PART A

In recent years, some people have developed the impression that immoral behavior exists only among individuals in the private, for-profit sector. This impression was reinforced by the failures of two major corporations.

- Enron Corporation was an energy-trading company. Using questionable accounting practices, it manipulated its earnings to disguise large losses. Its bankruptcy in 2001 was a major corporate failure brought about by fraudulent practices.

- Global Crossing is a major telecommunications company. It filed for bankruptcy in 2002 amid accusations that company executives made personal fortunes while shareholders lost billions of dollars.

## PART B

**Question:** Are leaders in government and the nonprofit sector immune to immoral behavior?

## PART C

**Answer:** Unfortunately, no. Moral failures exist among leaders in business, government and the nonprofit sector:

- In 2005, 17 Chicago government officials were under indictment for corruption in a truck-hiring program and for gross abuses in the city's contracts for minority and women-owned businesses.

- In 2005, 52 Florida government workers were arrested for selling thousands of commercial driver's licenses to illegal drivers.

- In 2006, federal officials alleged that 14 employees and others associated with the Red Cross stole donations intended for victims of Hurricane Katrina. Officials charged 49 suspects in the theft of about $200,000.

- In 2006, the financial manager of the Salvation Army in New Jersey was charged with embezzling more than $385,000 from the organization between 1995 and 2002.

**Moral:** No sector of society is immune from human failings. Improving the moral character of people in all walks of life makes society work better.

# VISUAL 4.2
# THE MARKETS AND ADAM SMITH'S INVISIBLE HAND

## PART A

Many people are skeptical of market systems. They fear markets may foster values that are harmful to society such as
- discrimination.
- dishonesty.
- excessive competition.

## PART B

**Question:** Many economists view markets differently. They say that markets generally contribute to the social good, not evil. Can you think of reasons why markets might serve the interests of society?

## PART C

**Answer:** Within a basic system of justice, competition forces businesspeople to consider the interests of others if they are to succeed. A business cannot make a profit if it ignores the desires of consumers, who make up 70 percent of the economy.

This concept is brought home by a famous quote from Adam Smith, considered the founder of economics:

[Every individual] neither intends to promote the public interest, nor knows how much he is promoting it . . . . [H]e intends only his own security; and by directing that industry in such a manner as its produce may be of the greatest value, he intends only his own gain, and he is in this, as in many other cases, led by an invisible hand to promote an end which was no part of his intention." (Adam Smith, *The Wealth of Nations*, eds. R.H. Campbell and A.S. Skinner, Indianapolis: Liberty Press, 1981 [1776], 456)

# VISUAL 4.3
# THE ECONOMICS OF DISCRIMINATION

## PART A

You are the manager of the Bigger Box Discount Store, and you want to hire a new worker in the food-service department to manage the popcorn concession.
  • You will pay the worker a wage of $10.00 an hour.
  • You charge consumers $1.20 for a bag of popcorn. After deducting the cost of the popcorn, you will have $1.00 left over to pay the worker and earn a profit.
  • The new worker must make and sell an average of 10 bags an hour for the popcorn concession to break even.

## PART B

**Question:** You have two candidates for the job: Which candidate will you hire and why?
  • A man the same race and age as you who can make and sell eight bags of popcorn an hour
  • An older woman whose ethnic background is clearly different from yours and who can make and sell 20 bags of popcorn an hour

## PART C

**Answer:** If your goal is to maximize profits, you will accomplish this by hiring the worker who makes and sells 20 bags an hour. To the profit-motivated manager, it is profit — not race, age or gender — that provides a basis for decision making. In general, businesses run for profit have an incentive to hire the most productive workers regardless of race, gender, age or religion.

## PART D

Government faces no consideration of profit when it makes hiring decisions.

## VISUAL 4.4
## MARKETS AND RACIAL DISCRIMINATION

Markets cannot solve all of society's problems, including rampant discrimination. Sometimes, however, the profit motive can lead businesses to play a role in creating new opportunities for the disadvantaged.

For example, between 1874 and 1964 various state and local laws in Southern states required segregation of the races. During this "Jim Crow" era, almost all public places including schools and transportation systems were required to maintain separate facilities for whites and blacks. But Southern streetcar owners early in the 20th century refused to discriminate against African Americans because discrimination reduced their profits.

One manager complained that Jim Crow segregation laws increased costs because the laws required the company to "haul around a good deal of empty space that is assigned to colored people and not available to both races."

African Americans boycotted streetcar lines that obeyed the laws and discriminated against them. Some African Americans formed competing horse-drawn carriage companies.

In Augusta, Savannah, Atlanta, Mobile and Jacksonville streetcar companies refused to enforce segregation laws for as long as 15 years after the laws were passed.

But one by one, the companies succumbed as government pressure for segregation grew and began to outweigh the costs imposed by the penalty on profits.

In 1954, the U.S. Supreme Court declared in *Brown v. Board of Education* that segregation in public schools was unconstitutional. Other segregation laws were repealed with passage of the Civil Rights Act of 1964.

Source: Jennifer Roback, "The Political Economy of Segregation: The case of segregated streetcars," *Journal of Economic History*, 56, no. 4 (December 1986): 893-917, as adapted in "Discrimination" by Linda Gorman in *The Fortune Encyclopedia of Economics*, edited by David R. Henderson (New York: Warner Books, 1993).

VISUAL 4.5
LIMITATIONS OF MARKETS

Competitive markets can provide incentives that work against discrimination. However, markets have sometimes contributed to discrimination:

American professional baseball was once characterized by rigid racial segregation. Some owners hired only white players because of long-standing racial prejudice. Other owners feared fans would react negatively at the box office if they hired nonwhite players, so discrimination existed for economic reasons.

Nonmarket factors also influence people's behavior: Some business owners may value their social status more than profits. These owners might condone racial or gender discrimination even if discrimination reduces their profits.

Moral norms and values are influenced by many institutions:
- competitive markets
- families
- religions
- schools
- voluntary organizations

## ACTIVITY 4.1
## FOUNDATIONS OF MARKET VALUES

**Directions:** Read the information below and be prepared to discuss the key points with the class.

Modern market systems operate within an institutional setting that protects private-property rights. Because of this, competitive markets must rely on voluntary exchange rather than force. Market systems also permit individuals wide freedom to make their own choices.

Yet markets do not operate in isolation. In a modern economy the "rules of the economic game" are established by a system of justice, which secures the type and scope of property rights. For example, the 13th Amendment to the U.S. Constitution, passed in 1865, profoundly altered property rights in America by eliminating slavery (ownership of another person).

To Adam Smith, justice "is the main pillar" that upholds society. In a modern market system, the first economic freedom is that each person owns himself or herself. Therefore, slavery, murder, rape and theft are unjust because they violate private-property rights. Since it is unlawful to take or destroy the property of others without their permission, individuals must engage in voluntary exchange to acquire the goods and services they desire. Market economies encourage us to serve the needs of others in order to receive the resources that will fulfill our own desires.

Economist Deirdre McCloskey identified many of the positive virtues that market systems foster. The content on the next two pages was influenced by her ideas. One major reason for the differences between market and nonmarket values is that markets are based on self-interested behavior and voluntary exchange. Markets create incentives that encourage you to serve others in order to benefit yourself.

## ACTIVITY 4.1 (continued)
## FOUNDATIONS OF MARKET VALUES

**COMPETITIVE MARKET VALUES**

**Discipline:** By stressing self-interested behavior, market systems encourage individuals to discipline themselves to produce the goods and services others want. Producing the goods and services demanded by others is rewarded.

**Honesty and Trustworthiness:** While market systems are susceptible to occasional scams and schemes, most businesspeople recognize that being honest and trustworthy with their customers will benefit their business over the long term. Customers will not continue to buy goods and services from people who cheat and lie to them.

**Tolerance:** Market systems tend to reward people who make good business decisions rather than decisions based on race, religion, gender, sexual orientation and other nonbusiness factors — in other words, people who judge employees on merit and sell to all customers who want to buy.

**Cooperation:** Cooperation is seldom identified as a basic characteristic of market systems. But market systems require substantial cooperation to produce the extraordinary achievements that we regard as ordinary. For example, how does a car with parts from 10 countries, hundreds of suppliers and thousands of distributors come to be sold in small towns? The act of producing and distributing cars (and other goods) requires extensive cooperation among strangers.

**NONMARKET VALUES**

**Discipline:** Nonmarket systems depend on tradition or force to encourage individuals to produce the goods and services others want. Failure to produce can lead to loss of respect or to miserable living conditions.

**Honesty and Trustworthiness:** Nonmarket systems rely on tradition or force to encourage people to be honest and trustworthy. Tradition and force often prove to be unsatisfactory, and over the long term people become inclined to trust only family members and friends. It is hard to maintain business relationships when customers can't influence the behavior of firms.

**Tolerance:** Nonmarket systems rely on tradition or force to encourage individuals to be tolerant — if these systems encourage tolerance at all. Here, too, tradition and force often prove to be inadequate or worse: People may use tradition and force in support of hatred, or hatred may be unleashed as soon as external constraints are relaxed.

**Cooperation:** Nonmarket systems rely on tradition or force to encourage individuals to work together. Joseph Stalin, for example, deliberately distributed manufacturing and agricultural enterprises across the former Soviet Union to force people from diverse ethnic backgrounds to cooperate with each another. As soon as the threat of force was removed under Mikheil Gorbachev, the Soviet Union collapsed. Cooperation created by coercion lasted for decades, but it could not be sustained.

# ACTIVITY 4.1 (continued)
# FOUNDATIONS OF MARKET VALUES

## COMPETITIVE MARKET VALUES

**Courtesy:** Market systems encourage people to be courteous because it is in their self-interest to be courteous. Customers do not like to deal with businesspeople who are rude or disrespectful. Some are rude or disrespectful anyway, of course — as long as they can hold onto their jobs or keep their businesses afloat. But over the long term, markets reward civil behavior, and businesspeople seek these rewards.

**Enterprise:** Market systems provide large rewards for inventive and innovative business leaders. People who are not afraid of change and willing to take risks are materially rewarded. As a result, new goods and services appear continually.

**Responsibility:** With their emphasis on self-interested behavior, market systems tend to focus on the individual and individual actions. The threat of individual failure is sobering, and it tends to encourage people to act responsibly.

**Accountability:** Markets provide people with both the incentives and information to be accountable to the concerns of others. People can compare firms on the basis of the price and quality of their products.

## NONMARKET VALUES

**Courtesy:** Nonmarket systems depend on tradition or force to encourage individuals to produce and sell the goods and services others desire. In this context, indifference or antipathy toward consumers is a persistent problem. Security guards in communist countries were assigned to many department stores. The guards were not there to protect the stores against thieves. They were there to protect the store clerks from customers who often became outraged by the clerks' surly, hostile attitudes.

**Enterprise:** Nonmarket systems tend to reward people for following the rules. "Follow the manual" might be the motto. Following the manual rarely results in inventions or innovations.

**Responsibility:** Nonmarket systems depend on tradition or force to encourage individuals to act responsibly. Shirking and cheating are often respected. People who get caught may be faulted merely for not having been smart enough to shirk and cheat and get away with it.

**Accountability:** Nonmarket systems are less accountable because there are no profits and the government sets prices. People often have a difficult time obtaining information from the government.

Source: Deirdre McCloskey, "Bourgeois Virtue," *The American Scholar* (Spring 1994): 177-191

# ACTIVITY 4.1 (continued)
# FOUNDATIONS OF MARKET VALUES

**Directions:** Use the information in the reading to write the answers to these questions.

**1.** According to this reading, what is the first economic freedom in a modern market system?

**2.** Slavery is often regarded as a market institution. After all, it involved many of the characteristics of a market including ownership, prices and exchanges. Do you agree that slavery was a market institution? Explain your answer.

**3.** How might owning and operating a restaurant encourage values such as honesty, enterprise and courtesy?

**4.** How might owning and operating a shoe store encourage values such as tolerance and responsibility?

**5.** How does the construction of a new home encourage cooperation among strangers?

# Lesson 5 — What Are the Moral Limits of Markets?

*The students brainstorm ways to allocate a scarce good and then discuss the moral advantages and limitations of markets for solving resource-allocation problems.*

## OVERVIEW

### Economics

In a world of scarcity, competitive markets provide powerful incentives for companies to develop better products, find lower-cost methods of production and produce the goods and services consumers demand. Markets also promote voluntary cooperation, prosperity and freedom. In the absence of market failures such as externalities and public goods, markets promote efficiency.

### Ethics

Markets are efficient, but other things matter too; and some goals might be better served by imposing limits on markets. For example, loyalty and cohesion are very important to family and social groups, but these cannot be bought or sold. Concerns about justice and virtue also lead people to recognize markets have limits and not everything that can be for sale should be for sale — for example, votes, babies and grades. Most people recognize that good citizenship requires virtues in addition to self-interest.

## LESSON DESCRIPTION

The lesson begins with the students brainstorming ways to allocate a scarce good within a small group. Then they evaluate market and nonmarket mechanisms for allocating goods and services. This leads to a discussion of the moral limits of markets. The students then read and discuss an article by Paul Heyne, who examines moral criticisms of markets and explains why morality is necessary for markets to work. Finally, the students apply this information to debate the moral limitations of markets.

## CONCEPTS

Civic virtue
Coercion
Competition
Corruption
Efficiency
Markets
Scarcity
Self-interest

## CONTENT STANDARDS

3. Different methods can be used to allocate goods and services. People, acting individually or collectively through government, must choose which methods to use to allocate different kinds of goods and services.

5. Voluntary exchange occurs only when all participating parties expect to gain. This is true for trade among individuals or organizations within a nation, and among individuals or organizations in different nations.

## OBJECTIVES

The students will:
1. Evaluate market and nonmarket methods for allocating goods and services.

2. Describe and analyze the benefits of market transactions.

3. Describe and analyze the main arguments for the moral limitations of markets.

## TIME REQUIRED

75 minutes

## MATERIALS

1. Visuals 5.1 and 5.2

2. One copy of Activities 5.1 and 5.2 for each student

3. One candy bar or other desirable item that can be divided easily for each group (see Procedure 1)

## PROCEDURE

1. Divide the students into groups of three to five. Display a desirable object such as a candy bar that can be divided easily. You could also use a healthy nutrition bar, a coupon for five extra-credit points or a homework pass. Ask the class how many students would like to have this item today. Assure them that this is not a trick question. You are willing to give them the item and, indeed, each group will receive one of these items today.

2. Explain to the students that this item is scarce because it is limited and the students in the class desire it. Tell them scarcity is a condition we face in every aspect of our economic lives. Individuals and societies must devise ways to deal with this problem, which is exactly what the class will be doing today. Assure the students that you have only a limited number of items to distribute: one per group. There are no more, for example, hiding behind your desk.

3. Ask the students to brainstorm answers to this question: "What are the various ways you can think of for allocating this item in your group?" Emphasize that they should think creatively. Give them up to five minutes to brainstorm. Then ask the students to share suggestions from their brainstorming. Write the suggestions on the board. It is very important not to discourage any answers.

4. After you have gotten all the suggestions, write the name in parentheses of the type of allocation, such as rationing, lottery, first-come/first-served, favoritism, brute force and the market. Here are some examples:
   • Divide the item equally among all the students in the group. (Rationing)
   • Draw straws or roll dice to determine who gets the item. (Lottery)
   • Have a race and the winner gets the item. (Favoritism based on achievement)
   • Give the item to the student who is hungriest or has the lowest grades. (Favoritism based on need)
   • Give the item to the student with the highest grade. (Favoritism based on achievement)
   • Have a fistfight and the winner gets the item. (Brute force)
   • Allow one student to offer others in the group a cash payment for the item. (Market)
   • Give the item to the person who needs it most. (Favoritism based on need)
   • Give the item to the first person who asks for it. (First-come, first-served)
   If the students' suggestions don't cover all the allocation methods, elicit the missing ones so that all the methods are represented on the board.

5. Tell the groups that they will have five minutes to consider the positive and negative aspects of each allocation option and decide who in their group will get the item. For example, a positive aspect of rationing and a lottery is that both treat everyone equally; however, this may not be fair if some people did more to deserve the good. Also, these allocation methods do not encourage greater effort, since everyone in the group is treated equally, regardless of effort. A positive aspect of favoritism is that scarce goods can be allocated to the people who are most in need — for example, the poor. Favoritism creates opportunities for bribery, however, so the people who are most in need may never get the goods. A positive aspect of competitive markets is that firms produce goods efficiently and sell them to the people who

place the greatest value on them. But this method may exclude people who don't have the means to pay.

6. Ask a spokesperson for each group to explain which allocation method it used and how the group decided who would get the item. Which criteria were important in making the final decision: Fairness? Favoritism? Efficiency?

7. Distribute the items based on the groups' decisions. (**Note**: If a group decides to use brute force, you may want to intervene. If a group fails to make a decision in the time allowed, allocate the item by lottery.)

8. Tell the students that, just as they had to decide who would receive a scarce good, an economic system must determine which goods and services to produce, how to produce them and who receives them. People make millions of allocation decisions every day. Tell the students that all types of allocation methods are in operation in various ways in our society.

   For example, more than 70 percent of the U.S. gross domestic product is consumer spending: Markets and prices determine which goods are produced and who buys them. Then families generally allocate scarce goods by rationing (we divide pizza slices equally at the dinner table). While brothers and sisters sometimes fight over allocations, brute force is most often used by robbers or by pirates. Selective colleges use favoritism based on achievement to determine which students to admit. Most colleges also use a lottery to determine housing allocations on campus. Many popular dance clubs and restaurants use first-come/first served, which explains why popular attractions have long lines. In times of war, society has used lotteries to draft people into the armed forces. Some products are banned (rationing with zero distribution).

9. Give each student a copy of Activity 5.1. Review the situations in which societies use nonmarket allocation methods to deal with problems of scarcity. Point out that some market transactions are inconsistent with human dignity while others permit people to take unfair advantage of others *(coercion)*. Times of emergency tend to affect people emotionally, so fairness becomes a greater concern than efficiency. Some goods or services should be illegal even if a person can pay for them. Moral goods (love and friendship) and civic goods (votes) are degraded unless people give them freely without a price. It would be immoral to sell certain things such as babies or grades in the market.

10. Tell the students that there are problems with each of the nonmarket allocation methods discussed in Activity 5.1. For example, suppose one student, Frank, really loves rock climbing, while all the other students are indifferent to it. Distributing a rock-climbing trip by using a random lottery would likely produce waste if someone wins — say, Jody — who doesn't like climbing. Treating people fairly sometimes requires acknowledging differences. Most people would say that allowing Jody to sell the rock-climbing trip to Frank (using the market) is more fair and efficient (less wasteful).

    Ask the students: "How would allocating rock-climbing trips based on price (and not by lottery) alter the outcome?" *It would mean that someone who values the trip most highly (Frank) will likely get to go. If Frank does not have the money to pay for the trip, then a lottery gives him a slightly better chance this time. However, a market system provides Frank with the opportunity to earn the money he needs by working. The harder his effort, the greater his chance of going because he can control his work and determination, but he cannot control a lottery. So in the long run, a market system provides Frank with a more reliable method of being able to enjoy the things he values most.*

11. Ask: "Would it be fair to give everyone in this class the same grade regardless of performance? What effect would this have?" *It is not fair because the students who work hard receive the same grade as the students who do not. Grades no longer serve as an incentive to motivate behavior. Student effort and achievement would likely fall because they aren't rewarded.*

12. Ask: "How do prices and wages in the market similarly act as incentives to alter behavior?" *High prices encourage people to conserve and to discover alternatives. Workers' desire for higher wages encourages them to work harder and invest in education. If firms gave all workers the same pay, the workers would have far less incentive to be courteous to clients, to produce efficiently and to care about consumers' desires.*

13. Display Visual 5.1. Tell the students that in the United States we often use competitive markets to allocate resources because markets provide us with greater opportunities for enjoying rock climbing and other things we enjoy most. Markets reward effort and invention. Competitive markets can align personal interests with social interests because prices are the incentives that reward desired behaviors. Go over the moral and practical advantages of markets listed on the Visual for consumers and producers.

14. Tell the students they are going to explore in more detail the moral advantages and disadvantages of markets. Give everyone a copy of Activity 5.2. Tell the students to read it as homework and bring the answers to the questions to class the following day. (You could assign the essay as in-class reading, but this will take considerable time.) Paul Heyne wrote the essay as a defense of markets against many moral criticisms. He also explains why morality is necessary for markets to work.

15. Discuss the answers to the questions on Activity 5.2.
    **Question 1:** Is self-interested behavior the same as selfish behavior? Why? *Paul Heyne argues that it is true only if someone's interests are selfish. In fact, a person can benefit from markets only if he or she appeals successfully to the interests of others. (See Lesson 2 for an extended discussion of this topic.)*
    **Question 2:** Would competition end if the government allocated all goods and services instead of relying on markets? *Heyne argues that as long as there is scarcity, there will be competition. The real question is what forms competition will take. Allocating resources through government is usually more wasteful than using markets.*
    **Question 3:** Would an economy that banned money be more moral than an economy with money? *People are not motivated by money itself but by what money will buy. Money is the most effective way to adjust incentives. Money may tip the scales, but this does not mean that people are selfish or that they do everything for money.*
    **Question 4:** Are poor people better off in a market system or in a system dominated by government? *The author argues that the poor receive less income than the rich in a market system; but markets provide the greatest benefits to the poor, who are even worse off in a government-dominated system. This is because power is generally tightly controlled by a few. Poor people have not flourished in government-dominated societies.*
    **Question 5:** Why do some people give presents and not money on birthdays and holidays? *Markets are not as important in personal relationships, and giving gifts is a personal act. Love may be a purer motivation than self-interest, but love is not always present in all relationships. The advantage of the market is that it encourages social*

*cooperation when relationships are not personal.*

**Question 6:** In what ways do the impersonal transactions of the market promote social cooperation? *Examine the production and distribution of any product. Thousands of people may be involved, and they may have different cultures, languages and religions and live in different places. Because markets create incentives, impersonal market transactions have expanded our ability to provide each other with healthful food, comfortable shelter, rapid transportation, remedies against disease and a more comfortable life.*

**Question 7:** Why are moral principles necessary for markets to work effectively? *Markets depend on voluntary exchange. If you cannot trust others, it is difficult to make voluntary transactions. Although markets are impersonal, they reflect the moral foundations of a community.*

## CLOSURE

16. Display Visual 5.2 and discuss why the students agree, disagree or are uncertain about the statement, which supports moral limits of markets. In discussing the statement, focus on what these moral limits, if any, might be. Also discuss whether markets or alternatives to markets are more effective in promoting ethical standards in a society.

    • Are some goods and services too valuable to trust to markets? Which moral and civic goods are damaged or corrupted if people buy and sell them for money?

    • Which moral and civic virtues do markets promote? Would government do a better job of promoting ethical values in society with price controls and rationing? What are the moral limitations of government intervention?

**The bottom line:** Most people agree that competitive markets efficiently allocate private resources and foster social cooperation among people who don't know each other. Yet critics believe that in certain circumstances markets corrupt moral and civic virtues. The debate comes down to the morality of markets and the moral implications of alternatives to markets.

## ASSESSMENT

### Multiple-Choice Questions

5.1 Based on "Moral Criticisms of Markets," which of the following statements would Paul Heyne support?
    A. Markets promote selfish behavior.
    **B. Markets promote social cooperation among strangers.**
    C. People do everything for money.
    D. Competition corrupts society.

5.2 Which of the following statements is a moral criticism of markets?
    A. Markets promote an inefficient allocation of resources.
    B. Market transactions are voluntary.
    C. Markets are more coercive than governments.
    **D. Markets may corrupt civic virtues.**

5.3 Which of the following allocation methods is most efficient and most responsive to the preferences of consumers who have income to spend?
    A. First-come/first-served
    **B. Markets**
    C. Government
    D. A lottery

### Essay Questions

5.1 Karl Marx was the major proponent of communism (central planning by the government). A famous paraphrase of Marx is: "From each according to ability; to each according to need." Explain this quotation using moral theory. Do you think Marx was correct in condemning market activities? *Marx focused on communal bonds and obligations. He correctly noted that in social groups there is a strong instinct for fairness. Family groups, for example, practice his motto of providing to each member according to need and asking of each member according to ability. Marx made a mistake in extending this idea to the nation as a whole. Marx argued that people will work for the good of the country and that monetary incentives should not matter. Communism tried to ignore the role that markets play in spurring production and productivity among strangers. Competitive markets allow freedom for both consumers and producers and promote virtues of honesty and responsibility. Communist countries failed to significantly improve the economic conditions of their people. Most people were poor, and government leaders were rich. Central planning and state ownership of the means of production resulted in coercion, mismanagement of resources, widespread corruption and a huge loss of freedom. More people died from hunger and murder by government under communism than under any other ideology.*

5.2 List and explain the moral limitations of markets. Explain why you agree or disagree with these limits. *Competitive markets solve problems of efficiency for consumers with incomes to spend. Markets don't provide for people who don't have money. Markets also can't fund public goods such as national defense. Other things matter besides private efficiency. Primarily, these include behaviors that respect the duties and obligations we have to each other in close relationships or as members of groups. Additionally, society expects fiduciary duties toward people who are vulnerable. In times of crisis, society demands shared sacrifices as a duty of citizenship. The second part of the question is opinion; make sure the students support their opinions.*

## GOING FURTHER

**Markets and Morality:** For an article that discusses why markets are moral, see Peter J. Hill, "Markets and Morality," available online at http://www.perc.org/perc.php?subsection=10&id=820

**Moral Limits of Markets:** For an article that discusses the moral limits of markets, see Michael J. Sandel, "What Money Can't Buy: The Moral Limits to Markets." This article is one of the Tanner Lectures available online at http://www.tannerlectures.utah.edu/lectures.html (use the alphabetic index in the left column to search for Sandel).

**Brute Force in Allocation:** For an example of brute force being used in allocation, see "Three Nations Coordinate Flights to Spy on Malacca Pirates," *The Christian Science Monitor*, August 17, 2005, at http://www.csmonitor.com/2005/0817/p10s01-woap.html

**Paul Heyne:** Paul Heyne was a gifted economics teacher at the University of Washington whose textbook, *The Economic Way of Thinking*, went through nine editions between 1973 and 1999. In the textbook, he presented economics as a method of thinking rather than "bits and pieces of technique." In the introduction to the book, he asks students "to master a set of concepts that will help them think more coherently and consistently about the wide range of social problems that economic theory illuminates." Heyne died in 2000. In 2006 Prentice-Hall published a revised edition of *The Economic Way of Thinking* by Peter J. Boettke and David L. Prychitko.
• To hear Heyne's final lecture, "The Moral Critics of Capitalism," which he delivered at the University of Washington-Seattle on February 17, 2000, go to http://ia300113.us.archive.org/2/items/heyne/Paul_Heyne-last_lecture-2000_February_17.mp3
• To hear the question and answer session that followed Heyne's lecture, go to http://www.archive.org/details/paulheyne

VISUAL 5.1
USING MARKETS TO DEAL WITH SCARCITY

Competitive markets generally align personal interests with social interests. Here are the moral and practical advantages of markets:

**For consumers, competitive markets**
- promote freedom of individual choice.
- treat equally customers with the same ability to pay.
- use prices to encourage conservation.
- provide for a reliable supply of private goods.
- use prices to eliminate shortages and long lines.
- improve living standards by providing better products at lower prices.

**For producers, competitive markets**
- promote freedom of individual action.
- rely on voluntary actions, not coercion.
- reward creativity in problem solving.
- promote cooperative behavior globally.
- encourage moral virtues such as hard work, honesty and thrift.
- align self-interest with efficiency at satisfying consumer desires.

VISUAL 5.2
MARKETS AND VALUES

Is this statement true, false or uncertain? Why?

"If we primarily rely on market exchanges to allocate resources, we will lose the values necessary to maintain a humane and just society."

# ACTIVITY 5.1
# THE LIMITATIONS OF MARKETS

Family and community relationships are the glue that holds societies together. Everyone in the group is generally expected to treat everyone else fairly, to respect human dignity and to fulfill mutual obligations. Sometimes using prices to allocate goods may violate deeply held moral and civic norms. For example, civic goods such as votes are degraded unless people give them freely instead of selling them.

Society tends to use nonmarket solutions — rationing, first-come/first-served, favoritism and lottery — to deal with scarcity when community values other than efficiency are paramount. Here are some situations in which markets may not be appropriate to allocate goods and services.

**Close Personal Relationships:** Family members and close friends have duties and obligations to each other. Benevolence and fairness are voluntarily given and usually expected. Selling love or friendship to the highest bidder debases these concepts. In these circumstances, scarce goods are generally shared or allocated based on need.

**Social Groups:** Individuals in social or civic groups such as schools, clubs and places of worship in which identity is conferred by membership have duties and obligations to each other. Once someone is selected as a member of the group, he or she is usually accorded equality; fairness is demanded. In these situations, people usually allocate scarce goods by rationing or lottery.

**Times of Crisis:** During war, disaster or danger people are strongly reminded of their common membership in society. Society expects everyone to do his or her civic duty, to share and sacrifice for the common cause. No one, for example, should be allowed to buy his or her way out of a draft. In times of crisis, rationing is often employed to allocate scarce goods.

**Vulnerability:** In some transactions, one participant is vulnerable: a child, an elderly person or a sick person. These transactions may be exploitative rather than mutually beneficial. People in a community generally uphold a duty to protect the vulnerable, so society often regulates or prohibits market transactions that involve minors or others who are unable to make informed decisions.

## ACTIVITY 5.1 (continued)
## THE LIMITATIONS OF MARKETS

**Vices:** Society tends to discourage or even ban activities that are thought to degrade important institutions in society. The sale and purchase of sex through prostitution weakens family ties, the sale of grades demeans the educational system and the purchase of a prison parole diminishes confidence in the rule of law.

**Equality:** Social goals may include equal opportunity for all as a basic right of citizenship. This could require communities to raise and redistribute funds so that education, health care and other services can be allocated based on need, not ability to pay.

# ACTIVITY 5.2
# MORAL CRITICISMS OF MARKETS

By Paul Heyne
*The Senior Economist* 10, no. 4, (April 1995)

Economics is important because it explains how markets work. Many people have difficulty understanding the operation of markets because they suspect that markets are fundamentally immoral. This essay is an attempt to examine the principal moral misgivings about market systems that I regularly encounter in my teaching of economics.

Photo: University of Washington – Seattle

## Selfishness and Self-Interest

Perhaps the most common moral objection to market systems is the one that asserts that they are based on universal selfishness. Is that true? A distressing number of otherwise sensible economists have adopted the unfortunate practice of asserting that economic theory assumes selfishness on the part of all participants in the economic system. That is either flatly false or a completely unwarranted change in the meaning of the word "selfish." Economic theory assumes self-interested behavior.

Self-interested behavior is selfish behavior only if one's interests are selfish. We could avoid confusion on this score by saying that economic theory assumes people act to further the projects that interest them. Whether those projects are entirely or primarily selfish depends on what kind of people they are. We should probably be slow to judge. What do we really know about other people's motives? It is wise to remember when we condemn other people's motives that the only motives we know for certain are our own.

Do teachers behave selfishly — to take a group of people most of us know quite well? Were teachers selfish when they chose their profession? When they selected a field in which to specialize? When they chose the schools they attended? The schools at which they then taught? Are they being selfish when they prepare for classes or respond to the students' questions? The claim that behavior in markets is distinguished by selfishness makes no sense.

# ACTIVITY 5.2 (continued)
# MORAL CRITICISMS OF MARKETS

## Can Competition Be Eliminated?

Another common moral objection to market systems is the objection to competition, usually thought of by the critics as an interpersonal struggle for superiority. Economists view competition differently. They see it as a process — often a completely impersonal process — of trying to satisfy whatever criteria others are using to allocate scarce goods. Scarcity means that it is not possible for everyone to have as much as she or he would choose to have if she or he were not required to make any sacrifice to obtain it. Scarcity therefore necessitates rationing, which means allocation by some set of discriminatory criteria. It follows that competition is the unavoidable accompaniment of scarcity and will consequently be found in every human society, whatever the form of its economic organization.

The question is not whether we shall have competition, but what forms it will take. That will be determined by the criteria used to allocate scarce goods. In a market system, the criteria will be the ones chosen by the effective owners of the scarce goods. For reasons to be examined in a moment, the chosen criteria in a market system are usually monetary: people compete largely by offering to pay more money for what they want to obtain and by agreeing to accept less money for what they are trying to supply.

When governments impose price controls to prohibit rationing by money bids and set up alternative systems for allocating scarce goods, competition does not stop. It merely takes new and almost always more destructive forms. That is why neither socialism nor communism can end competition. Even a transformation of human nature would not eliminate competition. If everyone in the society became a saint, competition would still exist because the saints would be committed to different charitable projects, and they would consequently have to devise some (saintly) way to decide how many resources to allocate to each project. Nothing can abolish competition except the abolition of scarcity. And since time will be scarce as long as life is finite, the elimination of scarcity requires the abolition of mortality. Moral objections to market systems alleging that market systems foster competition rest largely on misunderstanding.

# ACTIVITY 5.2 (continued)
# MORAL CRITICISMS OF MARKETS

## People Do Everything for Money

The moral critics of capitalism will probably not be satisfied by these arguments, however. "In a market system," they might reply, "people are motivated primarily by money." And that is certainly true. But what does it mean? Suppose you are a teacher who has been asked to sponsor the debate club. You really don't want to do it, but you agree when you are offered an extra $200 a month in salary. Were you motivated in this case by the money? It would seem so. But what does that tell us? It does not tell us you are interested only or primarily in money, because money is always a means to some other ends. Suppose Ms. Demosthenes wants the money in order to increase her contributions to the local children's hospital, and she will be giving up her regular bowling nights in order to find the time. Mr. Cicero will use the extra money to buy himself a new set of golf clubs and will fund the time by preparing less carefully for his classes. Both Ms. Demosthenes and Mr. Cicero did it for the money, but what a world of moral difference we find in why and how they really did it.

No one except a miser wants money for itself. To say that people are motivated by a desire for more money says little more than that people are motivated by a desire for additional means with which to pursue the projects that interest them. Morally, there is nothing reprehensible — or praiseworthy — about doing something "for the money."

Those who object to the prominence of monetary incentives in market systems have seized upon an important point, but it is probably not the point they were intending to make. In a market system, people do things for all kinds of reasons, out of all kinds of motives — just as in any other kind of social system. What is unique about market systems is that in such systems people change their behavior largely for monetary reasons. This occurs not because market systems foster an obsession with money, but because the offer of additional money is by and large the most effective way to adjust incentives appropriately.

Let's engage in a little mental experiment. Suppose we were living in a moneyless economy, in which all exchange takes place by barter. How would we go about adjusting the supply to the demand for the various kinds of labor services that we want? Suppose we have too many people who want to drive buses, for

## ACTIVITY 5.2 (continued)
## MORAL CRITICISMS OF MARKETS

example, and too few people who want to service telephone lines? What could we do to get people out of the buses and up on the telephone poles? Remember that everybody is different. We could try to discourage potential bus drivers by emphasizing the heavy responsibility they bear for the safety of others; but this would be counterproductive for people who think that responsibility makes their job meaningful. We could try to

> "... the offer of additional money is by and large the most effective way to adjust incentives appropriately."

encourage people to train with the phone company by emphasizing the healthful effects of outdoor work; but this would be counterproductive for all those who associate outdoor work with temperature extremes and rainy weather. We could offer bus drivers less meat in exchange for their services and offer more meat in exchange for the services of those who maintain telephone lines; but this would not work with vegetarians.

The easiest way to persuade people whom you don't even know — and almost all of the social transactions in a market economy are with people we don't know — is to offer more (and less) money. Those who complain about the predominant role of monetary motives in a market system are almost surely confusing marginal motivation with total motivation. Money tips the scales. That's all. It tips the scales precisely because it is money, which provides generalized command over resources. In the absence of some universally accepted scale-tipper, we could not have a market economy. That means we could never have developed the extensive division of labor that has made us so wealthy. Our civilization depends on the fact that an ounce of monetary persuasion, because it reaches almost everyone, produces a tone of responsive action.

### An Uncaring System

Sometimes the language of the critics suggests that they are objecting not so much to the actions of individuals as to the goals or intentions of the system itself. In responding to this objection, we must keep in mind that a social system really doesn't have any goals or intentions. And that may be exactly what the critics find so objectionable. Market systems allegedly accept what emerges

## ACTIVITY 5.2 (continued)
## MORAL CRITICISMS OF MARKETS

from individuals' pursuit of their own interests and ignore the inequalities and injustices that this produces. Market systems are "uncaring."

Considered abstractly, that may be quite true. But market systems don't exist in abstraction; they are always part of a larger social system. And it is certainly not the case that societies relying extensively on market systems ignore inequalities and injustices. Individuals, private groups, and governments regularly use the wealth that market systems generate to provide many kinds of assistance to persons who have fared poorly in those systems. Has the repudiation of market systems in the twentieth century by some governments produced more social justice, however we choose to define that slippery notion, than one finds in societies with full-fledged market systems? The poor receive less income than the rich in a market system; but the rise of market systems has arguably conferred its largest benefits on the poor, making the poverty of those who are least well off under a market system the envy of people in societies where markets have not flourished.

### Personal and Impersonal Transactions

Are there then no legitimate reasons to entertain moral misgivings about a society in which people alter their behavior primarily in response to changes in monetary incentives? Consider the following story.

You and your neighbor are mowing your lawns on Saturday morning. Suddenly he collapses in pain. You help him in the house and call the doctor. It turns out he has strained a muscle in his back. You go outside, finish mowing your lawn, and then finish the mowing of his lawn. That evening his wife comes over to tell you Jack is feeling much better and is very grateful for your help. She then hands you a $20 bill which she says Jack wants you to have for mowing his lawn. How would you feel? Probably stunned. Embarrassed as well. Even insulted. Why? Because what you did was done out of friendship and personal concern. It wasn't done for money, and the offer of money asserts that you and Jack are not friends.

It's not the fact that Jack is offering you something in return that bothers you. Suppose his wife had handed you a box of chocolates that you knew cost even

## ACTIVITY 5.2 (continued)
## MORAL CRITICISMS OF MARKETS

more than $20. You might be a bit embarrassed. You would say, "that isn't at all necessary." But you would not be insulted, because the chocolates are a personal gift in a way that money is not. Money is peculiarly impersonal.

But that is its chief virtue! Precisely because of its impersonality, we can use money to facilitate mutually advantageous transactions among millions of people who know little or nothing about one another personally.

> **"We obtain the help of others by appealing . . . to their self-interest."**

When we want pizza while traveling through a town we've never visited before, we just step into a pizza place, order a medium thin with sausage and green peppers, and in ten minutes we're eating pizza. We don't have to find a pizza purveyor who likes something we're carrying in the trunk of our car, or who would appreciate an hour or so of the labor services in which we happen to have specialized, or who is willing to provide us with a pizza because he shares our religion or admires our politics. We do our thing in return for money, he does his thing in return for money. We can each promote the interests of the other very effectively because we both value money.

Adam Smith observed early in *The Wealth of Nations* that, in a market society, everyone "stands at all times in the need of the cooperation and assistance of great multitudes," and that we cannot expect to obtain cooperation or assistance exclusively from their benevolence because life is too short for any of us to gain the friendship of more than a handful of other persons. We obtain the help of others by appealing not to their benevolence but to their self-interest. And we do that by offering them money. The institution of money enormously expands the number of people on whose assistance we can reliably count, by enabling us to gain the cooperation not just of friends but of millions of people we have never even met. In the absence of money, almost all social cooperation would have to be on a personal basis. In a market society, which is necessarily a monetary society, the social cooperation that provides all of us with most of what we need or want is predominantly impersonal.

For most of us, impersonal social relations arouse moral misgivings. We believe it is better, from an ethical standpoint, to provide others with pizza because we

# ACTIVITY 5.2 (continued)
# MORAL CRITICISMS OF MARKETS

know them, know what kind of pizza they like, and want to see them happy, rather than to provide the pizza because we want their money. That looks like using them for our own purposes, and we have ethical qualms about using people as means to our ends. The very phrase "using someone else" expresses these moral misgivings.

But in a market society, most interpersonal transactions are also impersonal transactions. The food we eat has been grown by farmers who make their planting decisions not with an eye on the appetites and nutrition needs of others, but with both eyes on the bottom line. Those who supply our food neither know nor care about our weight, cholesterol level, tastes, or values. And it's a good thing they don't. For if the farmers of the world decided not to produce for profit any longer but to satisfy human needs, and if they consequently went off to the cities to find out what people really need and want so that they could perform all their work on a personal basis, within a very short period of time most of the world's population would die of starvation.

We tend to suppose, quite wrongly, that the only genuinely ethical relationships between people are personal relationships. We consequently have deep moral misgivings about the very transactions that have made our civilization possible — the impersonal transactions that constitute the market system and that have, over the course of a few centuries, enormously expanded our ability to provide one another with healthful food, comfortable shelter, rapid transportation, remedies against disease, the discoveries and accomplishments of natural science, books in profusion, recorded music, and everything else that goes into our so-called "standard of living" — while at the same time vastly extending our freedom both by offering us a multitude of options and by freeing us from arbitrary restrictions on our choice of life goals and on the means to further those goals. To reject impersonal transactions as unethical amounts to rejecting the foundations of modern life.

There have in fact been massive experiments in this [twentieth] century with societies committed to the abolition of "commodity production" — the Marxian term for the organization of production through the impersonal transactions of the market system. If history ever pronounces "final verdicts," it pronounced one in 1989 on these experiments. Market systems do not produce heaven on

# ACTIVITY 5.2 (continued)
# MORAL CRITICISMS OF MARKETS

earth. But attempts by governments to repress them have produced in the twentieth century something very close to hell on earth.

## The Moral Foundations of Market Systems

The overwhelmingly impersonal character of market transactions and hence of a society dominated by market transactions does nonetheless present genuine moral issues. Markets generate powerful centrifugal forces in society by making individuals increasingly independent of specific other individuals. In a market society, Adam Smith correctly observed, everyone requires continual assistance from others. But not from any particular others. Those others are interchangeable. It is this feature of market systems that enables participants to be highly interdependent and yet at the same time highly independent.

The pressing question is how much independence a market system can tolerate. An effective market system presupposes some degree of community: at least enough community to provide consensus on basic rights and obligations. In a society where there is no commitment to such fundamental moral principles as equality of all before the law; where the civic virtues of tolerance and respect for others cannot be assumed; where fear of external authority is the only constraint on behavior because public opinion is not respected; where self-respect is not an effective force because society no longer presents a mirror in which the self can be observed — in such a society markets will not function satisfactorily.

If this analysis is correct, then defenders of market systems should themselves become to some extent moral critics of market systems. For the market requires moral foundations which cannot be created by market transactions themselves. Moral foundations are nurtured in communities — in families, neighborhoods, religious fellowships, local political associations, and other voluntary groups. By fostering the steady disintegration of these communities, market transactions may tend over time to undermine the moral foundations upon which they rest. That in itself is sufficient reason for those who place high value on the maintenance of market systems to remain in dialogue with the moral critics, who constantly remind us that a moral consensus is essential to every society and that its nurture and preservation is not a task that can safely be left to the market alone.

# ACTIVITY 5.2 (continued)
# MORAL CRITICISMS OF MARKETS

## Questions

**1.** Is self-interested behavior the same as selfish behavior? Why?

**2.** Would competition end if the government allocated all goods and services instead of relying on markets?

**3.** Would an economy that banned money be more moral than an economy with money?

## ACTIVITY 5.2 (continued)
## MORAL CRITICISMS OF MARKETS

**4.** Are poor people better off in a market system or in a system dominated by government?

**5.** Why do some people give presents and not money on birthdays and holidays?

**6.** In what ways do the impersonal transactions of the market promote social cooperation?

**7.** Why are moral principles necessary for markets to work effectively?

# Lesson 6 — What Should We Do About Sweatshops?

*The students learn three approaches for dealing with moral problems and then use these approaches to analyze the ethical dilemmas in sweatshops.*

## OVERVIEW

### Economics

Sweatshops are often portrayed as the horrifying underbelly of the global textile and apparel industries. This lesson explains what a sweatshop is and distinguishes between two different types: one operating in a competitive labor market and the other in a coercive labor market. Each has different economic and ethical implications.

### Ethics

We can analyze sweatshops on the basis of ethical outcomes, ethical duties and ethical character or virtues. One of the compelling ethical arguments against sweatshops is that, in some cases, they deny workers the minimum basic treatment that all human beings should receive. This lesson explains why this result is often not the fault of markets but of inadequate systems of justice.

## LESSON DESCRIPTION

This lesson introduces the students to three main ways of analyzing moral problems. The students apply these approaches to evaluate sweatshops. First, the students discuss the elements that make up a sweatshop. Then they read an essay on economics and ethics that defines sweatshops, and discuss the reasons why sweatshops exist. Next the students answer questions that reinforce their knowledge of the structure of labor markets. They consider two opposing views about sweatshops and discuss the ethical implications of sweatshops for the workers themselves and for consumers in wealthier countries. Finally, the students discuss and evaluate three policy options for dealing with sweatshops.

## CONCEPTS

Competition
Duty-based ethics
Exploitation
Gresham's law
Human rights
Justice
Outcomes-based ethics
Virtue-based ethics

## CONTENT STANDARDS

5. Voluntary exchange occurs only when all participating parties expect to gain. This is true for trade among individuals or organizations within a nation, and among individuals or organizations in different nations.

9. Competition among sellers lowers costs and prices, and encourages producers to produce more of what consumers are willing and able to buy. Competition among buyers increases prices and allocates goods and services to those people who are willing and able to pay the most for them.

10. Institutions evolve in market economies to help individuals and groups accomplish their goals. Banks, labor unions, corporations, legal systems, and not-for-profit organizations are examples of important institutions. A different kind of institution, clearly defined and enforced property rights, is essential to a market economy.

13. Income for most people is determined by the market value of the productive resources they sell. What workers earn depends, primarily, on the market value of what they produce and how productive they are.

## OBJECTIVES

The students will:
1. Identify the economic causes of sweat-shops.

2. Distinguish two main types of sweatshop labor markets.

3. Describe three ethical approaches that people use to analyze moral problems.

4. Apply these ethical approaches to a discussion of sweatshops.

5. Evaluate three policy options for dealing with sweatshops.

## TIME REQUIRED

90 minutes

## MATERIALS

1. Visuals 6.1, 6.2, 6.3 and 6.4

2. One copy of Activities 6.1, 6.2 and 6.3 for each student

3. Three posters or sheets of paper. Write "Treaty" on one, "Market" on the second and "Take No Action" on the third.

## PROCEDURE

1. Tell the students that this lesson will help them understand what sweatshops are and how to evaluate them.

2. Explain that many people react to sweat-shops without understanding the compet-ing economic and ethical considerations. Ask the students to write a few sentences that describe what they think a sweatshop is. Discuss their descriptions.

3. Display Visual 6.1.
   **A.** Discuss the workplace conditions that, in combination, make a factory a sweatshop. Tell the students that the mere presence of a condition does not necessar-ily constitute a sweatshop. A low wage,

for example, is not a sufficient reason to condemn a workplace. Otherwise, firms could not hire teenagers for summer work or part-time employment. The conditions listed on the Visual become abusive and result in a sweatshop when they occur in combination, are taken to an extreme and last a long time.
   **B.** Go over the list of contributing fac-tors. Make sure the students understand the impact of these factors on the work-place environment.

4. Distribute a copy of Activity 6.1 to each student. To save class time, you may assign this as homework reading. Tell the students to write the answers to the questions and be prepared to discuss their answers in class.

5. After the students have finished answer-ing the questions, ask: "How would econo-mists define a competitive labor market? How would they define a less-competitive labor market?" Display Visual 6.2 and go over the characteristics of each mar-ket. Emphasize that economists use the structure of a market as a key factor in determining the outcome of the market process — that is, to determine prices and quantities. In this case, the outcome is the wage rate and the number of workers that companies hire.

6. Discuss the answers to Questions 1 through 4 in Activity 6.1.
   **Question 1:** What is exploitation? What characteristics make a relation-ship in the labor market exploitative? *Exploitation means workers are paid less than their productive contribu-tions and are prevented from seeking better options. Exploitation can occur when only one business is hiring labor in an industry or a geographic area. It can also occur if businesses col-lude to keep out competition or gain control over labor from government. Exploitation can persist only if worker search costs are high, migration is*

*restricted and there are high barriers to entry of new firms. In essence, this exchange is coercive because other alternatives have been artificially blocked.*

**Question 2:** Are low wages in factories proof that firms are exploiting workers? Why? *No. A competitive market can result in low wages when the supply of labor is large relative to the demand. It is difficult for firms to exploit workers for very long in competitive markets because a productive yet underpaid worker will find better opportunities with other firms in the long run.*

**Question 3:** What key institutions may be missing in countries with less-competitive labor markets? *Countries with exploitative labor markets often don't have basic institutions of justice, a free press and representative government. Another key institution — competitive markets — is also typically missing.*

**Question 4:** How do labor markets in developing countries become more competitive? *Improvements in education, transportation and communication allow workers to more easily find better opportunities for themselves or their children. Removing government barriers that discourage competition and improving systems of justice are also important steps to improving the lives of poor workers.*

7. Display Visual 6.3. Tell the students that the table shows three ethical approaches people use when they debate public-policy issues such as sweatshops. Discuss these key points with the class:

• Economists generally use the outcomes-based method of analysis. Being a good economist means examining not only what is visible (sweatshops) but also what may be invisible (extreme poverty in rural areas). For example, a rural worker probably won't have other job opportunities, so working in a sweatshop would be her best choice to improve her standard of living.

• Other ethical approaches enrich our understanding by drawing attention to what makes society civilized and just. The U.S. Declaration of Independence, for example, asserts that all human beings are endowed with certain "unalienable" rights. We have moral duties to other human beings regardless of the repercussions or consequences.

• Most parents want their children to develop good character traits. Most religions strive to teach virtuous conduct. Philosophers from Aristotle to Adam Smith emphasize character. Do sweatshops deprive workers of opportunities to develop excellence in their characters? Or, alternatively, do sweatshops offer opportunities for poor people to practice a work ethic and build character? Nobel laureate economist Milton Friedman notes that his immigrant family's success began when his mother was able to land a job in a New York City sweatshop.

8. Go over the answers to Questions 5, 6 and 7 in Activity 6.1.

**Question 5:** Which of the following features of sweatshops is most troubling from the perspective of virtue-based ethics?

A. Workers receive very low wages.

***B. Workers do not have leisure or freedom to develop their characters.***

C. Sweatshops exploit the desperate situation of their workers.

D. Workers are not treated with respect.

**Question 6:** A duty-based approach to ethics settles moral decisions by

A. weighing the consequences of an act.

B. considering the greatest net pleasure that results from a particular decision.

***C. appealing to universal rules.***

D. considering the decision maker's character and intentions.

**Question 7:** An outcomes-based approach to ethics judges actions by

***A. weighing the consequences for society.***

**B.** considering what maximizes one's own happiness.
**C.** appealing to basic human rights.
**D.** considering the decision maker's character and intentions.

9. Tell the students that they will read contrasting perspectives on the sweatshop experience. Distribute Activity 6.2. Ask the students to read it in class and write the answers to the questions.

10. When the students have finished, divide the class into groups of four or five students. Have one-third of the groups prepare to argue Question 1 from an outcomes-based perspective, one-third from a duty-based perspective and one-third from a virtue-based perspective. Allow five minutes for preparation. Give each group one minute for its presentation. Ask for and allow rebuttals from other groups.

**Question 1:** Sweatshops make it possible for wealthy consumers in developed countries to buy cheap products. Does this beneficial outcome make sweatshops morally justifiable? Why? Include in your answer the moral perspective from which you are arguing. *Answers will vary. Make sure the students understand the relevant ethical approaches. Tell them they don't always need to give each approach equal weight or consideration, but they should come to understand that all three approaches offer perspectives on why some economic issues are so controversial. Critics of capitalism often use nonoutcomes-based arguments that economists find difficult to understand. It is not necessary for the students to think that each ethical approach should always be given equal weight or consideration.*

*An outcomes-based approach focuses on consequences. The outcome of low prices for U.S. consumers is a beneficial result. Even though pay in sweatshops is low, sweatshops create job opportunities in poor countries at higher wages than workers received before.*

*Duty-based ethicists argue that inhumane workplace conditions violate basic human rights. So the "good" outcome for U.S. consumers and higher wages for poor workers are irrelevant because something more important is at stake. According to this view, the economic process must respect basic human dignity and human rights.*

*Virtue-based ethicists aren't concerned with cheap prices of consumer products but with the development of character. Cheap products might simply contribute to materialism and the degradation of important cultural values. Sweatshops may not be consistent with the opportunity for people to develop a virtuous character.*

11. Discuss the answers to Questions 2 and 3 in Activity 6.2 with the students.

**Question 2:** If Americans refused to buy products made in countries that have sweatshops, who would benefit? Who would be hurt? Why? *If production of the products moved to the United States, owners of U.S. factories would benefit. American consumers would be hurt because they would pay higher prices. Workers in developing countries would be hurt because they would be unemployed or employed under worse conditions. If countries made less economic progress, the standard of living would be lower for their current and future citizens.*

**Question 3:** What can people in developed countries do to improve working conditions in developing countries? *Answers will vary and may include supporting monitoring of factories, promoting more world trade and competition, providing certification of manufacturing operations through trade organizations and providing aid to improve the infrastructure and environment of developing countries.*

12. Display and discuss Visual 6.4 as background for Activity 6.3. The Visual describes the Fair Labor Association's Workplace Code of Ethics and lists some participating companies. As of October 2006, FLA-certified manufacturers covered 3,500 factories around the world. Use this information to help the students understand the market solution to sweatshops in Question 5 on Activity 6.3.

13. Tell the students that they will evaluate and vote on three specific policy options for dealing with sweatshops. Distribute Activity 6.3 and have the students read it and write the answers to the questions. Then discuss the answers.

   **Question 1:** If a treaty similar to the Geneva Convention established minimum working conditions in labor markets, what basic rights should the treaty provide for every worker around the world? *Answers will vary and may include the right to safe working conditions, freedom from physical or mental intimidation, regular toilet breaks, a maximum work day (for example, 12 hours), a maximum work week (for example, six days) and the right to organize union or choose not to join one.*

   **Question 2:** What are the difficulties of requiring firms to pay all workers around the world a "living wage"? *In some competitive labor markets, firms may pay a low wage because of low productivity. An imposed "living wage" is a price floor, which causes a surplus of labor. Attempting to force a higher wage will simply result in workers losing their jobs. It is also next to impossible to determine what a living wage is. Many entrants to the labor market live with family members and can survive on a low wage. Others cannot, so paying a living wage to all employees would require firms to pay unequal wages to workers with equal skills.*

   **Question 3:** In the United States, the Fair Labor Standards Act of 1938 sets basic working conditions that include restricting child labor and requiring companies to pay employees a minimum wage and overtime if they work more than 40 hours a week. Should all other countries be required to match these standards? Why? *Determining the minimal conditions for employment is highly subjective. It is ethnocentric to assume that the standards of one country are perfect for all others. European countries have much stronger labor regulations than the United States, for example. The key problem is that many countries with sweatshops are very poor. The United States had many sweatshops when it was poor. It is problematic to say a poor country should have the same labor regulations as a richer country.*

   **Question 4:** What are the advantages and disadvantages of using treaties to establish workers' rights? *Advantage: There is a level playing field for factories in all countries. Disadvantages: The countries with the worst labor conditions cannot be forced to sign the treaty. In addition, unless there is some mechanism of enforcement, a treaty could lack effective "teeth": Signing it would make a country look good but perhaps produce little change. Regulations also impose costs on businesses. When regulations are excessive, government regulators can be bribed, leading to greater corruption in society.*

   **Question 5:** What are the advantages and disadvantages of using the market-monitoring approach to reform sweatshops? *Refer the students to Visual 6.4 if they need help understanding the market solution to sweatshops.*

   *Advantages: Businesses listen to consumers. If people insist on improved labor conditions before they buy a product, companies would quickly adapt. This approach is noncoercive, relying instead on the business's own profit motive.*

   *Disadvantages: In order for con-*

*sumers to react to sweatshop conditions, there must be a free press (or other mechanism) to report abuses. Even if consumers are informed, they may not be interested in sweatshops. Certification programs cost apparel makers money, which would likely mean higher prices for consumers. Many companies use subcontractors to provide textile products, and there may be a lack of transparency in these arrangements. Finally, different certifying organizations may have contradictory standards (for example, whether there should be a living wage), making it difficult for both producers and consumers. Manufacturers may feel intimidated or blackmailed by certifying organizations, which may have the ability to put them out of business.*

**Question 6:** What are the advantages and disadvantages of using the take-no-action approach to reforming sweatshops? *Advantages: An action might harm sweatshop workers. Foolish acts motivated by good intentions may not make things better, and could make things worse. When the United States was poor, it had many sweatshops. Economic growth, along with social legislation, fixed the problem over time. Clearly, people should be alert to the dangers of ethnocentrism and moral relativism when they evaluate each opportunity for intervention in overseas affairs. Disadvantages: If moral conscience is deeply aroused, doing nothing seems a morally intolerable solution. Standing by to watch human-rights abuses can be a short-sighted approach. Doing nothing may result in capitalism developing a bad image, and this could result in much stricter government controls and intrusion later. One can never have perfect information, so requiring perfect information before acting guarantees only paralysis.*

14. Tell the students they will vote on their preferred policy regarding sweatshops. Remind them that critical thinking means weighing arguments and reaching an independent conclusion for themselves. Place on the floor three large posters or sheets of paper with "Treaty" written on one, "Market" on the second and "Take No Action" on the third. Ask the students to stand near the poster with the policy they find most convincing and briefly explain why they selected this option. *Answers will vary based on the previous discussions.*

## CLOSURE

15. Help the students understand that economic and moral problems are usually more complex than they first appear. Explain that simplistic solutions create their own sets of problems. The role of an economist is to see what is hidden as well as what is visible. An economist can help assess costs and benefits using an outcomes-based approach. Other ethical approaches based on duty and virtue help people evaluate important issues and thereby create a better society.

**The bottom line:** Sweatshops exist because of economic and other conditions. If a sweatshop is profitable, the pursuit of profit will eventually lead to imitation and rivalry, pushing up wages if the market is competitive. When there is a large influx of unskilled workers from rural areas, however, this process can take decades.

Pursuing other ethical approaches can improve some factory conditions but not others and may create new complications such as higher unemployment. A key problem in many countries is the lack of a fair system of justice.

## ASSESSMENT

### Multiple-Choice Questions

**6.1.** Which of the following is NOT a characteristic of sweatshops?

    *A. Sweatshops are workplaces that always earn high profits.*

    B. Sweatshops are factories where people work long hours under unhealthy or unsafe working conditions.

    C. Sweatshops are workplaces where people can be subjected to intimidation and violence.

    D. Sweatshops are workplaces that do not treat workers with dignity.

**6.2.** Sweatshop conditions are often said to result from

    A. a transparent working environment in which outsiders can monitor conditions.

    B. the tendency of people to work together, no matter how bad the conditions may be.

    *C. a large rural population, heavy population density and high rates of poverty.*

    D. the tropical climate of some workplaces.

**6.3.** According to an economic view, exploitation is a condition that arises in what type of labor market?

    A. Markets with a lot of competition

    B. Markets with fewer workers than the number of available jobs

    C. Markets with many employers

    *D. Markets with little competition*

### Essay Questions

**6.1** Do sweatshops prove that firms exploit workers in developing countries? Why? *Not necessarily. Owners of firms are seeking profits, and employees are seeking the best available opportunities. In circumstances of extreme poverty and massive unemployment, a low wage is not proof of exploitation. While the market wage and benefit package can be barely suf-ficient to sustain life, it is sometimes all that keeps families alive. Corrupt, weak and undemocratic governments may also fail to protect the poor. Exploitation occurs in less competitive labor markets when employers collude to set wages or use violence to intimidate the flow of labor or restrain the entry of new opportunities for labor. Such situations illustrate that markets can work for the benefit of people and society only when a country has an effective and fair system of justice. Consumers can also more easily ignore the conditions in exploitative sweatshops if poverty keeps workers nameless and faceless.*

**6.2** Analyze the advantages and disadvantages of three policy options regarding sweatshops. Which solution do you favor and why? *The three options could be: a) a global treaty, b) market monitoring and c) doing nothing. The advantages and disadvantages of each are addressed in the answers to the questions in Activity 6.3.*

## GOING FURTHER

### Do Your School's Sweatshirts Come from Sweatshops?

• Have the students visit their school store and try to identify where the school T-shirts and other apparel items are made. Do the labels identify the country of origin? Does the school shop participate in any factory-certification group such as the Fair Labor Association or the Worker Rights Consortium? Why?

• Many university shops adhere to one or more certifying codes. For a discussion of one school's policies, see Northwestern University's approach to licensing at http://www.univsvcs.northwestern.edu/trademark/fla_wrc.htm

**Certification Associations:** A number of third-party groups, many of which are nonprofit organizations, have been created to monitor human-rights violations related to factories. Have the students visit the Web site of one of these groups and find a copy of its code of con-

duct or ethics.
- Fair Labor Association
(http://www.fairlabor.org)
- Worker Rights Consortium
(http://www.workersrights.org/)
- Collegiate Licensing Company
(http://www.clc.com/clcweb/publishing.nsf/
Content/Home.html)
- Ethical Trading Initiative
(http://www.ethicaltrade.org/)

**Research a Company:** Have the students
visit the Fair Labor Association's Web site and
research a particular country or company.
(For a list of company participants, go to http://
www.fairlabor.org/all/companies/index.html)
If possible, have the students interview a company executive to discuss the business perspective on certification programs.

**Additional Resources:** For general information and additional readings on the sweatshop
debate, have the students visit two academic
Web sites devoted to this issue:
- In opposition to sweatshops: Scholars
against Sweatshop Labor (SASL)
http://www.umass.edu/peri/sasl
- In support of sweatshops: Academic
Consortium on International Trade (ACIT)
http://www.fordschool.umich.edu/rsie/acit

## VISUAL 6.1
## FEATURES OF SWEATSHOPS

### Workplace Conditions
- Low wages
- Long work hours
- Health and/or safety hazards
- Arbitrary discipline by managers or owners
- No job security
- Physical abuse, threats and intimidation
- Workers have no voice in government
- Child labor

(**Note:** These conditions result in a sweatshop when they occur in combination, are taken to an extreme and last a long time.)

### Contributing Factors
- Dense populations
- Limited education
- High unemployment
- Few job alternatives
- Extreme poverty
- Workers with low productivity
- No social safety net
- Corrupt, weak or undemocratic government
- Secrecy and lack of workplace transparency, often in places without a free press
- No system of justice to protect basic rights
- Consumer ignorance about or neglect of the plight of sweatshop workers

# VISUAL 6.2
# MARKET STRUCTURES

## COMPETITIVE LABOR MARKET

### Characteristics
- Many buyers of labor
- Many sellers of labor
- Free entry or exit
- Voluntary exchange
- Good information for both buyers and sellers

### Economic Prediction
Firms are forced to pay the equilibrium wage determined by supply and demand. Wages reflect workers' contributions; otherwise, workers who feel exploited are able to find better jobs.

## LESS-COMPETITIVE LABOR MARKET

### Characteristics
- One buyer of labor or collusion of several buyers acting as one
- Many sellers of labor
- Entry of competing firms blocked
- High costs for workers to search for jobs
- Coercive exchange because other job options for workers are artificially blocked
- Asymmetric (one-sided) information or bargaining power

### Economic Prediction
Wages are set below competitive equilibrium. Firms exploit workers because they pay the workers less than the value of their marginal contributions. Exploitation can persist if workers have trouble finding other jobs and problems in the justice system aren't resolved.

# VISUAL 6.3
# APPROACHES TO ETHICAL ISSUES

| Ethical Approach | To Determine Whether Sweatshops Are Helpful or Harmful | Consider |
|---|---|---|
| Outcomes matter. (Outcomes-based ethics) | Examine the outcomes in people's lives | • Impact on workers' standard of living <br> • Opportunity costs |
| Duty matters. (Duty-based ethics) | Ask whether the basic dignity of all human beings is upheld. The process, particularly whether anyone's human rights are violated, is key. | • U.S. Declaration of Independence <br> • Geneva Convention for Treatment of Prisoners of War |
| Character matters. (Virtue-based ethics) | Decide whether sweat-shops contribute to the formation of good character and virtues for workers, managers and consumers | "The superior person understands what is moral. The small person understands what is profitable." <br> — Confucius |

# VISUAL 6.4
# THE MARKET APPROACH:
# APPAREL-INDUSTRY CERTIFICATION

Many consumers would like to buy products made under acceptable working conditions. One way to provide this information is for independent associations to certify factories that meet basic standards.

The Fair Labor Association (FLA) is one apparel-industry certification group. Participants include Adidas-Salomon, Eddie Bauer Inc., Gear for Sports, Gildan Activewear, Nike, Outdoor Cap, Patagonia Inc., Phillips-Van Heusen Corp., Puma, Reebok International and 194 colleges, universities and secondary schools in the United States and Canada with more than 1,900 licensees.

FLA members agree to abide by the association's Workplace Code of Conduct, which prohibits
- forced labor, including prison labor
- child labor
- physical, sexual, psychological and verbal harassment and abuse
- discrimination on the basis of gender, race, religion, age, disability, sexual orientation, nationality, political opinion or social or ethnic origin
- unsafe and unhealthy working conditions

The code also requires participants to
- recognize and respect the right of employees to bargain collectively
- pay employees the local or industry minimum wage
- provide workers with legally required benefits
- maintain reasonable hours of work and give employees one day off each week
- pay employees for working overtime

# ACTIVITY 6.1
# SWEATSHOPS AND LABOR MARKETS

**Directions:** Read the information in each section, and write the answers to the questions. Be prepared to discuss your answers with the class.

What are sweatshops? In general, sweatshops are factories that operate under poor working conditions — arguably in violation of basic human rights. These conditions may include the use of child labor, health and/or safety hazards, extremely low wages, excessively long hours, arbitrary discipline, physical abuse, threats and intimidation. A sweatshop does not necessarily exist if one or two of these conditions are present for a limited period, but a factory is a sweatshop if it has a persisting combination of many of these characteristics.

Sweatshops sometimes exist in developed countries, including the United States, but they are most common in less-developed nations, particularly in Asia and Latin America. Textile and apparel factories supply goods to larger corporations, many of which are household names. These larger companies sell the goods to consumers. To keep the companies' business, factories must often compete fiercely with each other on the basis of price.

Are low wages in factories proof that workers are exploited? To answer this question, economists study the structure of markets and ask some key questions: How many buyers of labor are in the market? How many sellers? Is there free entry and exit? Do workers have options?

## COMPETITIVE LABOR MARKETS

A competitive labor market is characterized by a number of firms separately and independently bidding for the services of labor. Experimental data indicate that the number of firms in the market need not be large, as long as the firms bid independently. Likewise, workers separately and independently compete for jobs. The equilibrium wage rate is the wage that clears the market so that supply and demand are balanced.

Low wage rates can exist in competitive labor markets that have high levels of poverty and unemployment and a lack of education. Low wages are a sign that workers have low skill levels and low productivity. Workers can seek jobs from employers that pay more, but until the workers improve their skills, natural forces will hold down wages.

# ACTIVITY 6.1 (continued)
# SWEATSHOPS AND LABOR MARKETS

## LESS-COMPETITIVE LABOR MARKETS

A less-competitive labor market is characterized by only one firm or by a cartel of firms bidding together for labor. Without the force of competition, employers can set wage rates below a worker's worth, artificially holding wages down. Exploitation occurs when employers pay workers a wage below the true value of the workers' contributions as measured by their productivity.

In the early history of capitalism, workers frequently feared — and often faced — collusion among employers. Collusion can include blacklisting workers who try to switch jobs or form unions. This caused Adam Smith, the founder of modern economics, to write that anyone who doubts employers collude "is as ignorant of the world as of the subject." Smith went on to say that employers in his day "are always and everywhere in a sort of tacit, but constant and uniform combination . . . . to sink the wages of labour . . . ." (Adam Smith, *The Wealth of Nations*, eds. R.H. Campbell and A.S. Skinner, Indianapolis: Liberty Press, 1981 [1776], 84) The formation of labor unions was a natural response to this.

Smith's solution to collusion was to promote active and open competition, which forces employers to pay workers the market value of their labor. Most workers in developed countries have access to the Internet, cell phones and fast transportation. Thus they have the ability to take their labor to the highest bidder. But modern labor markets can still lack competition for several reasons:

## 1. Workers face high search costs.

Most of the world's poor are illiterate and live in rural areas. Such factors make it difficult for these workers to search for better opportunities. Additional factors may contribute to this problem:
  • Communication and roads are inadequate, and workers lack motorized transportation. Unless workers migrate away from their families, their daily job search is limited to the area they can reach on foot in two or three hours.
  • In many Latin American countries, land ownership is highly concentrated. It is difficult for rural workers to find competing employers. Workers still have the option to migrate. However, rural families may be in permanent debt to the landowner, who also owns the local store. Workers in these families cannot leave without facing arrest, yet staying means getting deeper in debt (and debts are transferred to children).
  • Asymmetric (one-sided) information or bargaining power may exist. Workers may be unaware of labor laws that provide certain rights such as minimum wages, limited

## ACTIVITY 6.1 (continued)
## SWEATSHOPS AND LABOR MARKETS

hours and rest breaks. Employers may prevent workers from forming unions to counter the bargaining power of the firm.

- Finally, employers have used violence to intimidate workers and members of the press who attempt to raise questions about coercive labor conditions.

### 2. Competitive firms cannot enter.

A firm with monopoly power in the labor market can block others from entering if the firm owns all the land in a region and refuses to sell. A business can also use political power to limit competition in the labor market. This occurred in the Philippines under President Ferdinand Marcos when the government gave a company run by the president's close friend an exclusive contract to buy copra, the juicy meat of coconut. ("Mr. Marcos's 'Capitalism,'" *The Wall Street Journal*, July 1, 1985) Companies or government officials can also use intimidation and violence to discourage competitive firms from entering the market.

### JUSTICE AND COMPETITION

Countries in which companies do not compete for workers probably don't have basic institutions of justice and democratic representation. In these countries, businesses control the levers of justice, and no rule of law protects citizens from arbitrary acts. According to Adam Smith, justice is the "main pillar" without which society would "crumble into ashes" (Adam Smith, *The Theory of Moral Sentiments*, eds. D.D. Raphael and A.L. Macfie, Indianapolis: Liberty Press, 1982 [1759]). Smith was a strong supporter of markets as a mechanism for helping the poor rise out of poverty. But for markets to help, there must first be institutions of justice. The government itself must be made to follow the rule of law. Workers must also have a voice in governing the nation through a fair vote on its laws.

# ACTIVITY 6.1 (continued)
# SWEATSHOPS AND LABOR MARKETS

**Questions**

1. What is exploitation? What characteristics make a relationship in the labor market exploitative?

2. Are low wages in factories proof that firms are exploiting workers? Why?

3. What key institutions may be missing in countries with less-competitive labor markets?

4. How do labor markets in developing countries become more competitive?

# ACTIVITY 6.1 (continued)
# SWEATSHOPS AND LABOR MARKETS

## ETHICAL APPROACHES TO PROBLEMS

In Western society there are three main ways of analyzing ethical problems: outcomes, duty and character.

## ETHICAL APPROACHES TO SWEATSHOPS

| Ethical Approach | To Determine Whether Sweatshops Are Helpful or Harmful | Consider |
|---|---|---|
| Outcomes matter. (Outcomes-based ethics) | Examine the outcomes in people's lives | • Impact on workers' standard of living <br> • Opportunity costs |
| Duty matters. (Duty-based ethics) | Ask whether the basic dignity of all human beings is upheld. The process, particularly whether anyone's human rights are violated, is key. | • U.S. Declaration of Independence <br> • Geneva Convention for Treatment of Prisoners of War |
| Character matters. (Virtue-based ethics) | Decide whether sweatshops contribute to the formation of good character and virtues for workers, managers and consumers | "The superior person understands what is moral. The small person understands what is profitable." <br> — Confucius |

# ACTIVITY 6.1 (continued)
# SWEATSHOPS AND LABOR MARKETS

**Questions**

**5.** Which of the following features of sweatshops is most troubling from the perspective of virtue-based ethics?

    **A.** Workers receive very low wages.

    **B.** Workers do not have the leisure or freedom to develop their characters.

    **C.** Sweatshops exploit the desperate situation of their workers.

    **D.** Workers are not treated with respect.

**6.** A duty-based approach to ethics settles moral decisions by

    **A.** weighing the consequences of an act.

    **B.** considering the greatest net pleasure that results from a particular decision.

    **C.** appealing to universal rules.

    **D.** considering the decision maker's character and intentions.

**7.** An outcomes-based approach to ethics judges actions by

    **A.** weighing the consequences for society.

    **B.** considering what maximizes one's own happiness.

    **C.** appealing to basic human rights.

    **D.** considering the decision maker's character and intentions.

# ACTIVITY 6.2
# TWO PERSPECTIVES ON SWEATSHOPS

**Directions:** Read the two perspectives on sweatshops and write the answers to the questions. Be prepared to discuss your answers with the class.

## PERSPECTIVE 1

### Anh Tien and the Harmony Delight Company
By Martin Calkins, University of Massachusetts-Boston
(**Note:** This is a fictional case study based on accounts of real-life experiences.)

Anh Tien is a 16-year-old girl from a farming village in Vietnam. Bright and industrious, Anh has worked hard since she was a small child on one of the local farms. However, a prolonged drought caused Anh to lose her job, and there are few other opportunities in the isolated rural area. Complicating matters, her grandmother became ill, and Anh felt increasing pressure to contribute financially to her family.

Anh's friend, Linh Nguyen, came to visit the village one day. Linh had recently moved to the city and found a job in a porcelain factory. She told Anh about the city and the people streaming into it from rural villages such as theirs. Linh said the city was a tough place, but she was glad to have found a job since jobs were scarce. Her work was demanding, but not nearly as bad as the work in a textile factory that she heard about. Anh decided to leave and take Linh's offer to stay at Linh's place in the city until she could find work.

Anh's first days were most unpleasant. The filth, noise, smell and press of the crowds were nearly overwhelming. She saw beggars everywhere and groups of loitering young people. Anh preferred to stay indoors, but Linh's roommates objected to her constant presence. One even suggested that Anh look for work at Harmony Delight Company, the textile manufacturer with the horrible work conditions. With no other job prospects, Anh decided to check out Harmony Delight.

Anh walked into Harmony Delight and was greeted by a surly man who turned out to be the foreman. He asked what she wanted, and Anh replied that she was looking for work. The foreman said Harmony Delight did not have anything for her. As she started to walk away, the foreman said, almost in passing, that the factory might need someone to attend to one of the spinning lines. Anh jumped at the prospect and soon found herself in front of a large contraption.

Her job was simple: She had to make sure the threads coming out of the machine were untangled. The job was easy to understand, but demanding. Anh was not

## ACTIVITY 6.2 (continued)
## TWO PERSPECTIVES ON SWEATSHOPS

allowed to sit down, and she was in constant contact with the material the machine produced. Within a few hours, Anh was covered in fiber and tired of standing. Her hands were red and sore from the friction of the moving threads, and she had to go to the bathroom. Knowing she should not leave the machine unattended, Anh asked the foreman to give her a break. His response took her by surprise: She could not leave her workspace and could use the bathroom only during her short lunch break. In great discomfort, Anh remained at her post.

In late afternoon, Anh thought quitting time must be at hand. Her feet and back were aching, her fingers were blistering and her eyes were puffy from the airborne fiber. As darkness set in, however, there was no move to end work. It was 11:00 p.m. when the foreman finally dismissed Anh for the day. He told her to reappear, ready to work, at 7:00 a.m. She dragged herself to Linh's apartment and collapsed on the space on the floor that she called her own.

The next day Anh arrived at Harmony Delight at 7:00 a.m. To her surprise, there was a line of people at the gate looking for work. She immediately realized these people wanted her job, so she scurried to her post, feeling grateful. Her gratitude, however, was soon replaced by the same numbing fatigue she experienced the previous day.

As days and weeks wore on, Anh pushed herself to become a steady employee six days a week. She worked seven days when times were particularly tight back home. Her $2-a-day wage could buy food or medicine for her grandmother. Although she was only 16, Anh had circles under her eyes, and her hands were as calloused as those of the old farmers back home. She had seen things at the factory she never would have imagined. The foreman regularly beat laggards. Sometimes the air was clouded with fiber. Anh had heard the dust could explode if one of the machines emitted a spark. Although she wasn't making much money, her income was better than no income at all. And she always saved enough to send something to her family to keep them from starving. If only she could sit down once in awhile.

# ACTIVITY 6.2 (continued)
# TWO PERSPECTIVES ON SWEATSHOPS

**PERSPECTIVE 2**

**Two Cheers For Sweatshops** (excerpt)
By Nicholas Kristof and Sheryl WuDunn
*The New York Times*, September 24, 2000
©2000, Nicholas Kristof and Sheryl WuDunn, reprinted with permission.

Nothing captures the difference in mind-set between East and West more than attitudes toward sweatshops. Nike and other American companies have been hammered in the Western press over the last decade for producing shoes, toys and other products in grim little factories with dismal conditions. Yet sweatshops that seem brutal from the vantage point of an American sitting in his living room can appear tantalizing to a Thai laborer getting by on beetles.

The truth is, those grim factories in southern China contributed to a remarkable explosion of wealth. Wages have risen from about $50 a month to $250 a month or more today. Factory conditions have improved as businesses have scrambled to attract and keep the best laborers.

In fact, the most vibrant parts of Asia are nearly all in what might be called the Sweatshop Belt, from China and South Korea to Malaysia, Indonesia and even Bangladesh and India. Today these sweatshop countries control about one-quarter of the global economy. As the industrial revolution spreads through China and India, there are good reasons to think that Asia will continue to pick up speed. Some World Bank forecasts show Asia's share of global gross domestic product rising to 55 to 60 percent by about 2025 — roughly the West's share at its peak half a century ago. The sweatshops have helped lay the groundwork for a historic economic realignment that is putting Asia back on its feet.

Of course, it may sound silly to say that sweatshops offer a route to prosperity, when wages in the poorest countries are sometimes less than $1 a day. Still, for an impoverished Indonesian or Bangladeshi woman with a handful of kids dying of mundane diseases like diarrhea, $1 or $2 a day can be a life-transforming wage.

In Cambodia, a large mosquito net costs $5. If there had been a sweatshop in the area, however harsh or dangerous, [many young girls] would have leapt at the chance to work in it, to earn enough to buy a net big enough to cover all her children.

## ACTIVITY 6.2 (continued)
## TWO PERSPECTIVES ON SWEATSHOPS

Sweatshop monitors do have a useful role. They can compel factories to improve safety. They can also call attention to the impact of sweatshops on the environment. The greatest downside of industrialization is not exploitation of workers but toxic air and water. In Asia each year three million people die from the effects of pollution. The factories springing up throughout the region are far more likely to kill people through the chemicals they expel than through terrible working conditions.

By focusing on these issues, by working closely with organizations and news media in foreign countries, sweatshops can be improved. But refusing to buy sweatshop products risks making Americans feel good while harming those we are trying to help. As a Chinese proverb goes, "First comes the bitterness, then there is sweetness and wealth and honor for 10,000 years."

**Questions**

**1.** Sweatshops make it possible for wealthy consumers in developed countries to buy cheap products. Does this beneficial outcome make sweatshops morally justifiable? Why? Include in your answer the moral perspective from which you are arguing.

**2.** If Americans refused to buy products made in countries that have sweatshops, who would benefit? Who would be hurt? Why?

**3.** What can people in developed countries do to improve working conditions in developing countries?

# ACTIVITY 6.3
# WHAT SHOULD WE DO ABOUT SWEATSHOPS?

**Directions:** Read the information below and write the answers to the questions. Be prepared to discuss the answers in class.

Any attempt to reform sweatshops through government regulation runs into Gresham's law: weak regulators will drive out strict regulators. Consider this example: If Vietnam established strong labor standards for protecting worker rights, this could lead textile companies to close factories in Vietnam and reopen them in Cambodia where regulations are weaker. Strict but piecemeal regulation of labor cannot succeed as long as capital is freely mobile.

## OPTION 1: INTERNATIONAL TREATY

One option is to have all countries agree on the rules of the economic game. This is the approach the World Trade Organization takes when its member nations negotiate international trade treaties — some of which include labor-market regulations. Countries have also used international treaties to establish a legal framework for environmental rules across national boundaries. The Geneva Convention is an example of a duty-based approach established by international treaty: Prisoners of war have the basic rights to food, shelter, health care, protection from torture and dignity.

### Questions

1. If a treaty similar to the Geneva Convention established minimum working conditions in labor markets, what basic rights should the treaty provide for every worker around the world?

## ACTIVITY 6.3 (continued)
## WHAT SHOULD WE DO ABOUT SWEATSHOPS?

**2.** What are the difficulties of requiring firms to pay all workers around the world a "living wage"?

**3.** In the United States, the Fair Labor Standards Act of 1938 sets basic working conditions that include restricting child labor and requiring companies to pay employees a minimum wage and overtime if they work more than 40 hours a week. Should all other countries be required to match these standards? Why?

**4.** What are the advantages and disadvantages of using treaties to establish workers' rights?

# ACTIVITY 6.3 (continued)
# WHAT SHOULD WE DO ABOUT SWEATSHOPS?

## OPTION 2: MARKETS AND MONITORING

Instead of using government regulations to reform sweatshops, consumers could "vote" their preferences by refusing to buy goods from companies that fail to provide acceptable working conditions. Since consumers may lack basic information about factory conditions, third-party groups (many of which are nonprofit organizations) have been created to determine where the goods are produced, inspect factories and monitor human-rights violations. Many university students took a role in this process by insisting that their schools buy apparel such as sweatshirts made only in approved factories.

By increasing the demand for certified apparel, the market provides an economic incentive for companies to voluntarily introduce better working conditions. For this option to be effective, business relationships must be transparent: Uncertified Factory A can't attach to its clothing an apparel tag from certified Factory B.

## Question

**5.** What are the advantages and disadvantages of using the market-monitoring approach to reform sweatshops?

## ACTIVITY 6.3 (continued)
## WHAT SHOULD WE DO ABOUT SWEATSHOPS?

**OPTION 3: TAKE NO ACTION**

A final approach is to take no action. Over the past 20 years, living standards have risen rapidly in countries where sweatshops help people overcome rural poverty. Interfering with the lives of strangers can have unintended negative consequences on economic, social and political processes. Noble intentions don't necessarily ensure excellent outcomes.

Ethnocentrism is the mistaken view that the customs governing your society should govern all societies. For example, if child labor is outlawed in a rich country, it should also be outlawed in a poor country. On the other hand, moral relativism is the equally mistaken position that all indigenous practices are morally valid.

**Question**

**6.** What are the advantages and disadvantages of using the take-no-action approach to reforming sweatshops?

# Lesson 7 — Should We Allow a Market For Transplant Organs?

*The students analyze four policies for dealing with the shortage of kidneys to transplant and debate the ethical strengths and weaknesses of the market solution.*

## OVERVIEW

### Economics

The sale of transplant organs is illegal in the United States. People may donate organs but not sell them. In other words, the price of transplant organs is set at $0 and below equilibrium. This price ceiling is causing a shortage. Repealing the law that prohibits the sale of body parts would alleviate the shortage because a higher market price would increase the quantity of organs supplied and decrease the quantity of organs demanded.

### Ethics

Public-policy analysis usually involves both ethical reasoning and economic analysis. Outcomes-based ethics, with its focus on the consequences of policies, tends to support a legal market for body parts. Duty-based and virtue-based ethics, by contrast, raise concerns about an open or modified market. Duty-based theorists focus on ethical principles or rules that should guide people's actions. Virtue ethicists focus on the personal qualities that enable us to do the right things that good people would do. The ultimate decision about organ sales requires people to make a judgment or to rank values or goals based on their ethical framework.

## LESSON DESCRIPTION

The students learn that there is a shortage of transplant organs in the United States. They explore ways to reduce the shortage, particularly by increasing the supply. First the students use supply and demand to analyze a market for kidneys. Then they learn how different ethical theories can help us evaluate policies for procuring organs to transplant. Finally, the students must decide which of four organ-transplant policy options they would support.

## CONCEPTS

Demand
Duty-based ethics
Equilibrium price
Incentives
Outcomes-based ethics
Price ceiling
Supply
Virtue-based ethics

## CONTENT STANDARDS

3. Different methods can be used to allocate goods and services. People, acting individually or collectively through government, must choose which methods to use to allocate different kinds of goods and services.

4. People respond predictably to positive and negative incentives.

7. Markets exist when buyers and sellers interact. This interaction determines market prices and thereby allocates scarce goods and services.

8. Prices send signals and provide incentives to buyers and sellers. When supply or demand changes, market prices adjust, affecting incentives.

## OBJECTIVES

The students will:

1. Describe the effects of a price ceiling on the market for kidneys available for transplant.

2. Analyze the effects of legalizing the purchase and sale of transplant organs.

3. Describe three main types of moral or ethical theories.

4. Use economic and ethical theories to evaluate four organ-transplant policies.

## TIME REQUIRED

90 minutes

## MATERIALS

1. Visuals 7.1 and 7.2

2. One copy of Activities 7.1, 7.2 and 7.3 for each student

3. Four posters or sheets of paper with "The Current System" written on one, "An Open Market" on the second, "A Regulated Market" on the third and "A Communitarian Approach" on the fourth.

## PROCEDURE

1. Explain to the students that they will analyze how to deal with a large and growing shortage of transplant organs in the United States. Because of this shortage, many people die while waiting for a transplant, and others must use expensive medical procedures and equipment to stay alive.

2. Display Visual 7.1 to describe the extent of the problem.

3. Tell the students that federal law prohibits buying and selling transplant organs. Only donated organs are acceptable. Some people suggest that the shortage would be alleviated if people could buy and sell organs for transplant. Although it may

sound macabre to pay for body parts, the opportunity to buy and sell organs would save lives and improve the quality of life for many people.

4. Give each student a copy of Activity 7.1. Ask the students to read the information and write their answers to the questions. (**Note:** The students must understand supply, demand, equilibrium and the effects of price ceilings to answer the questions.)

5. Display Visual 7.2 to illustrate the supply of and demand for kidneys. Give the students a general explanation of what the graph illustrates. Point out that although the data are hypothetical, the graph can help the students analyze current organ-donor policies and the effects of changing these policies.

6. Discuss the answers to the questions on Activity 7.1.

   **Question 1:** Federal law currently bans the sale of kidneys. This effectively establishes a maximum legal price for kidneys of $0. This is called a *price ceiling*. Because of the ban, doctors may use only donated kidneys for transplants. Based on the graph, how many kidneys will people supply (donate) for transplanting when the price is $0? *At a zero price, people will supply 20,000 kidneys; this is where the supply curve intersects the quantity axis.*

   **Question 2:** Why would anybody donate a kidney if the price is $0? *Some people donate kidneys to relatives and even to complete strangers at a price of $0. Others donate their organs after death. People make these donations because of altruistic motives and the nature of their characters; the donation has nothing to do with monetary rewards.*

   **Question 3:** Based on the graph, how many kidneys do patients demand when the price is $0? *At $0, all patients who need a kidney would be able to afford* one. *The quantity demanded will be 80,000; this is where the demand curve crosses the quantity axis.*

**Question 4:** The shortage in kidneys is the difference between the quantity demanded and the quantity supplied when the price is $0. Based on the graph, what is the amount of the shortage? What do you think caused the shortage? *The number of kidneys donated (20,000) is less than the quantity of kidneys demanded (80,000) when the price is $0. There is a shortage of 60,000 kidneys. The price ceiling caused the shortage.*

**Question 5:** In summary, how many kidney transplants will occur each year with the price ceiling of $0? How many patients will remain on the waiting list? *With a legal price of $0, there will be only 20,000 kidneys available for transplanting. This is the number of transplants. There will be a shortage of 60,000 kidneys, so 60,000 patients will remain on the waiting list.*

**Question 6:** Suppose the federal government repealed the law banning the sale of organs. If this were to happen, some consumers on the waiting list would begin to offer higher prices for a kidney. The market would eventually reach equilibrium where supply and demand curves intersect. At this equilibrium, what is the market price? What is the equilibrium number of kidneys people would buy? *The equilibrium of supply and demand occurs when the price reaches $30,000 a kidney. (For comparison you might tell the students that this is roughly the average price of a new car or truck.) At this price the quantity supplied is 50,000 kidneys a year and the quantity demanded is also 50,000 a year, so the market clears.*

**Question 7:** How has the rise in price affected the behavior of suppliers? To answer, compare the new equilibrium quantity with your answer to Question 1. Can you make any generalizations about the people who might sell a kidney at the equilibrium price but would not donate a

kidney when the price is $0? *The quantity of kidneys supplied would increase from 20,000 a year to 50,000 a year. Because a kidney is valuable, people who are poor and need more income are more likely to sell one of their kidneys. Other people may sell their kidneys after they die because the income to their heirs makes it worthwhile.*

**Question 8:** How has the rise in price affected the behavior of consumers (patients)? To answer, compare the new equilibrium quantity with your answer to Question 3. Can you make any generalizations about the people who might demand a kidney when the price is $0 but will not buy one when the price reaches equilibrium? *As the price rises from $0 to $30,000, the quantity demanded decreases from 80,000 to 50,000. Some people cannot afford a kidney at a higher price or will choose an alternative medical procedure — continuing on dialysis, for example — rather than paying for an organ.*

**Question 9:** According to the graph, how many kidney transplants would occur each year at the new equilibrium price? How much of a shortage exists at this price? *There will be 50,000 transplants a year. Since quantity demanded equals quantity supplied at equilibrium, the shortage is now zero. What this means is that everyone who was willing to pay the equilibrium price got to buy, and everyone who wanted to sell at this price got to sell. People who were willing to pay $30,000 would no longer be on the waiting list. However, there would still be patients needing a transplant who could not afford to buy at this price.*

**Question 10:** Assuming all other factors are constant, would a free market for kidneys result in more or fewer kidney-related deaths each year? *Fewer people would be at risk of dying while on dialysis because, with a free market, the number of transplants would increase from 20,000 to 50,000 a year.*

**Question 11:** Would a free market in kidneys be fair to poor people? Argue both sides of this issue.

*YES: A person needs only one kidney to live. The money a poor person would earn by selling a kidney can pay for college, a down payment on a house or other family needs. (A seller from a poor country might typically earn only $500 a year. This seller can make perhaps 60 times as much selling one kidney.) If it is legal and fair for people to sell hair and blood, it should be legal to sell kidneys.*

*NO: Poor patients who need a kidney transplant will be priced out of the market by wealthier buyers. Poor people who sell their kidneys may make illogical decisions about their own welfare and face serious health consequences later. Government should be paternalistic and refuse to let people make choices that may be harmful.*

**Question 12:** If the legal price of kidneys is very high, does this pose a risk to public safety: Is there an incentive for organ theft? *As with any valuable commodity, the higher the potential return, the higher the chance of theft. But the current price ceiling makes a stolen kidney infinitely valuable (assuming a thief could find a hospital and surgeon to transplant it). By contrast, a free market makes kidneys relatively more available and reduces the incentive for underground markets.*

**Question 13:** Do you think that either the supply or demand curve might shift if the government instituted a legal market for kidneys? If so, which curve would shift and in which direction? *The demand curve probably would not shift because demand depends on the wants, needs, income and alternative choices of the recipients. None of this would be changed by legalization. The supply curve might shift inward — toward the left. Supply could decrease at every price level because altruis-*

*tic donors might be less motivated to donate when people are selling organs.*

**Question 14:** Assume there was a successful campaign to encourage more donations of kidneys. How would this campaign shift the supply curve? How would this campaign affect the equilibrium price and quantity of kidneys? What would happen to the shortage of kidneys? *The supply curve would shift to the right or increase. The price would decrease and the equilibrium quantity of kidneys transplanted would increase. The shortage would decrease.*

**Question 15:** Is the graph for a market in kidneys realistic? Why? *It is realistic. The demand curve might be more inelastic than shown on the graph because receiving a kidney is a matter of life and death. However, demand would not be perfectly inelastic because at higher prices some potential customers could not afford to buy a kidney and because there are substitutes for receiving a kidney transplant.*

7. Conclude by asking: If it is obvious that a significant shortage of kidneys could be alleviated if we create a legal market for organ sales, why don't we just create one? *Answers will vary. Guide the discussion toward ethical considerations. In particular, should prices be used to allocate goods in life-or-death situations?*

8. Tell the students that they will now deal with these ethical considerations. Give each student a copy of Activity 7.2, and ask them to read it. Tell them not to answer the questions yet. When they have finished reading, summarize the three main types of ethical theories.
   • **Outcomes-based ethics** holds that the right action results in the best outcomes. Clearly, having more kidneys available for transplant is a good thing because it shortens the waiting list and saves lives.

The consequences in terms of fairness or unequal access to kidneys are not as clear.

  • **Duty-based ethics** is based on rules that help us do the right thing. Is it right to treat your body as a commodity? Why?

  • **Virtue-based ethics** asks what a good person would do. Would a good person sell or buy a kidney? Why?

9.  Ask the students to write the answers to the questions at the end of Activity 7.2 and then discuss the answers as a class.

**Question 1:** What are the advantages and disadvantages of an ethical theory that focuses on satisfying consumer preferences in a market? *The most difficult problem arises from a perception of fairness. As long as people believe income is distributed fairly, then the way people spend their income will be perceived as fair. Satisfying people's preferences makes many more kidneys available for transplanting and promotes individual freedom. The preference theory runs into problems when consumers prefer to buy things that society deems unacceptable such as drugs and pornography.*

**Question 2:** What are the advantages and disadvantages of using absolute ethical rules to determine public policy for kidneys? *The advantage is that you have a clear set of rules to guide your actions. However, this could lead to intolerance toward others who believe in different rules or who view consequences (for example, saving the most lives) as the most important criterion in implementing a policy.*

**Question 3:** How would you describe the ideal human character? How might your description affect your analysis of buying and selling kidneys? *Answers will vary. The discussion should make it clear that defining the ideal human character is not easy.*

**Question 4:** In considering the buying and selling of kidneys, which ethical approach influences you most? Why? *Answers should vary and focus on how*

*different ethical theories bring about different conclusions even if people agree on the facts.*

10. Give each student a copy of Activity 7.3, and ask them to read it. While they are reading the activity, put the four pieces of paper with the names of the policies on the classroom floor or on the three walls away from the door.

11. When all the students have finished reading, ask them to stand next to the policy they support. Then ask them to explain their position. *Answers will vary, and the students should support their position with ethical and economic theories. Here are some discussion points:*

  • *Supporters of outcomes-based ethics will probably support an open market or a regulated market for kidneys because they believe the outcome advances a number of worthy objectives: More lives are saved, people get to buy what they want with their incomes (efficiency in consumer preferences) and freedom is enhanced. Under some circumstances fairness to sellers is enhanced because poor people are allowed to market their kidneys at a high price. Some outcomes-based ethicists may judge fairness to buyers as an overriding concern. Patients with low incomes may suffer and therefore some outcomes-based ethicists may elect to stay with the current system or a regulated system rather than wide-open markets. A person who blends outcomes-based ethics with a duty-based approach could support a regulated market. Some outcomes-based ethicists would favor aspects of the communitarian option because it could increase the supply of donations.*

  • *Supporters of duty-based ethics may object to free markets in body parts because of the loss of dignity or sanctity implied in turning humans into commodities. They are concerned about the precedent that this may create in other markets such as adoption. They may also object to the presumed authoritarian consent option because of the loss of individual freedom (government using coercion to take body parts unless an individual makes a decision to the contrary). Duty-based ethicists may be influenced by religious beliefs. Some students, for example, may argue that it is wrong to sell kidneys because humans are created in the image of God.*

*• Supporters of virtue-based ethics would endorse the responsive communitarian approach of changing preferences through an ad campaign. If good people do good things, the impersonal forces of the market may not be necessary. Education can shape human character and increase the number of organ donations. Virtue ethicists argue that it is a mistake to treat love, benevolence and particularly public spirit as scarce resources that must be economized or they will be depleted. Unlike material factors of production, the supply of love, benevolence and public spirit may increase rather than decrease through use. Moral resources respond positively to practice, and atrophy through neglect.*

*• Virtue ethicists might oppose the authoritarian communitarian approach by saying a good person does not need to be coerced and might resent being forced to donate. However, according to "Can a Christian Be an Economist?" by Charles K. Wilber, University of Notre Dame, "a principal objective of publicly proclaimed laws and regulations is to stigmatize certain types of behavior and to reward others, thereby influencing individual values and behavior codes. Aristotle understood this: 'Lawgivers make the citizen good by inculcating habits in them, and*

*this is the aim of every lawgiver; if he does not succeed in doing that, his legislation is a failure.' "* (http://www.nd.edu/~cwilber/pub/recent/acexrist.html)

## CLOSURE

12. Ask why organ-donation policy is so difficult to develop. *Answers will vary, but buying and selling body parts has ethical implications that buying and selling most goods does not.*

**The bottom line:** Creating an open or regulated market for kidneys would help alleviate the shortage caused by current policy, which sets the legal price at $0. Creating a legal market would also reduce activities in an illegal market. However, ethical considerations make the decision to commodify body parts more difficult. An organ market offends the religious or personal beliefs of many people. Others fear that creating a market may turn off potential donors; they believe that ethical persuasion can change people's preferences.

## ASSESSMENT

### Multiple-Choice Questions

7.1 Which of these statements about a price ceiling is correct?
    A. A price ceiling causes a shortage if the ceiling price is above the equilibrium price.
    B. A price ceiling causes a surplus if the ceiling price is above the equilibrium price.
    *C. A price ceiling causes a shortage if the ceiling price is below the equilibrium price.*
    D. A price ceiling shifts the demand curve to the right.

7.2 If a legal market in kidneys for transplant replaced the current law forbidding the buying and selling of kidneys, what would happen?
    A. The price would rise, and the quantity of kidneys demanded would increase.

**B. The price would rise, and the quantity of kidneys supplied would increase.**

C. The shortage of transplant kidneys would increase.

D. The supply curve for transplant kidneys would shift to the right.

7.3 Which ethical theory would be most supportive of a legal, open market for kidneys?

A. *Outcomes-based ethics*
B. Duty-based ethics
C. Virtue-based ethics
D. Value-based ethics

## Essay Questions

7.1 Analyze the impact of the current federal law, which prohibits the sale of kidneys and allows only free-will donations. *This law creates a price ceiling at a price of $0. This price ceiling is below equilibrium and causes a shortage of kidneys available for transplant. The policy may also create an illegal market in which people sell kidneys at very high prices and quality is not assured. Finally, because there is a shortage, nonprice considerations such as health and age determine who receives a kidney. The shortage also has resulted in a lengthy waiting list for transplants.*

7.2 Before it was stopped, bidding for a kidney on eBay reached $5.7 million. Without considering the fact that buying kidneys is illegal, do you think the bidding should have been stopped? *This is an opinion question, but the opinion must be supported by economic and ethical considerations. A student who supports the bidding might see it as a step in alleviating the shortage. A free market is efficient, creates incentives to increase organ sales, reduces suffering and maximizes the ethical value of freedom. The initial high price would encourage others to offer*

*kidneys for sale, and the price would drop in the long run. People who want to stop the bidding might have religious or other ethical views that oppose the sale of human organs. They also could view the action as unfair to poor people or as creating a backlash so good people stop donating kidneys.*

## GOING FURTHER

**Current Kidney Data:** For data on kidney transplants and waiting lists, go to the United Network for Organ Sharing Web site at http://www.unos.org

**Underground Markets:** This lesson does not discuss one of the repercussions of price ceilings, which is that illegal or underground markets in kidneys would develop. For information on this topic, go to http://news.nationalgeographic.com/news/2004/01/0116_040116_EXPLorgantraffic.html to read "Organ Shortage Fuels Illicit Trade in Human Parts."

**Ethical Decision Making:** The Markkula Center for Applied Ethics at Santa Clara University has an excellent Web site for decision making when ethical dilemmas are present: http://www.scu.edu/ethics/practicing/decision/

**How to Increase Kidney Donations:** An alternative method of alleviating the kidney shortage is to increase the number of voluntary donations. For a discussion of this communitarian approach, see Amitai Etzioni, "Organ Donation: A Communitarian Approach" at http://muse.jhu.edu/journals/kennedy_institute_of_ethics_journal/toc/ken 13.1.html

VISUAL 7.1
ORGAN TRANSPLANTS: DEMAND EXCEEDS SUPPLY

Federal law prohibits buying and selling organs for transplant. In 2005:

- Doctors transplanted 28,000 organs in the United States — more than 21,000 from deceased donors and 7,000 from living donors.

- 6,000 patients died while waiting for a transplant.

- 91,000 patients were on a waiting list for transplants (all organs).

- The waiting list for transplants increased at twice the rate of donations.

- Survival rates for transplant recipients continued to increase.

Source: U.S. Organ Procurement and Transplantation Network, administered by the United Network for Organ Sharing. More recent data are available at http://www.optn.org/data

# VISUAL 7.2
# SUPPLY OF AND DEMAND FOR KIDNEYS

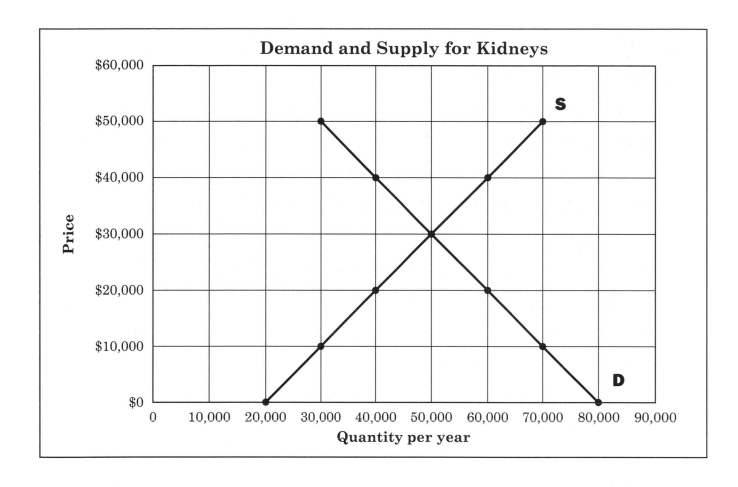

(Note: All data are hypothetical.)

## ACTIVITY 7.1
## A MARKET IN KIDNEYS

**Directions:** Read the information and write the answers to the questions.

In the United States about 60,000 patients are on a waiting list for a kidney. Many of these patients will die before receiving one. In this activity we will build a model to help us understand the nature of the kidney shortage. All numbers are hypothetical and for illustrative purposes only.

We start by examining the behavior of people who make kidneys available for transplanting. Kidneys are supplied for transplant in two ways:
- through people dying
- through living people giving up a kidney. Everyone has two kidneys and can survive on just one. Kidneys from living people are generally higher quality, and transplants with these kidneys tend to be more successful.

If people were allowed to buy and sell organs, here's what the hypothetical supply and demand curves for kidneys would look like:

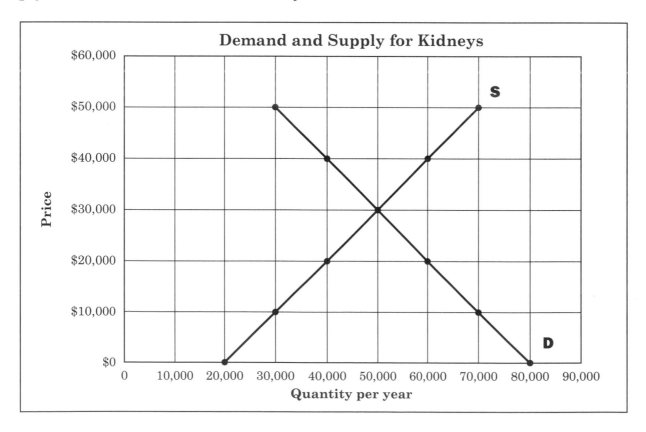

# ACTIVITY 7.1 (continued)
# A MARKET IN KIDNEYS

The supply curve (S) shows the relationship between the price and the quantity of kidneys available for transplanting each year. This is a positive relationship because the higher the price, the greater the number of living individuals who would willingly give up a kidney in exchange for money. While it may seem gruesome to sell an organ for money, many poor people would make this decision with the hope of bettering their lives.

The demand curve (D) shows the relationship between the price and the quantity of kidneys patients are willing and able to buy each year. This is a negative relationship because the higher the price, the fewer the number of individuals who would be willing and able to buy a kidney. It might seem that patients would be willing to pay any price for a kidney if the alternative is death. However, patients have limits on their income and wealth. While they might want to pay a high price, their circumstances may not allow it. Hence, the demand curve for kidneys would not be vertical (perfectly inelastic).

## Questions

**1.** Federal law currently bans the sale of kidneys. This effectively establishes a maximum legal price for kidneys of $0. This is called a *price ceiling*. Because of the ban, doctors may use only donated kidneys for transplants. Based on the graph, how many kidneys will people supply (donate) for transplanting when the price is $0?

**2.** Why would anybody donate a kidney if the price is $0?

## ACTIVITY 7.1 (continued)
## A MARKET IN KIDNEYS

**3.** Based on the graph, how many kidneys do patients demand when the price is $0?

**4.** The shortage in kidneys is the difference between the quantity demanded and the quantity supplied when the price is $0. Based on the graph, what is the amount of the shortage? What do you think caused the shortage?

**5.** In summary, how many kidney transplants will occur each year with the price ceiling of $0? How many patients will remain on the waiting list?

**6.** Suppose the federal government repealed the law banning the sale of organs. If this were to happen, some consumers on the waiting list would begin to offer higher prices for a kidney. The market would eventually reach equilibrium where supply and demand curves intersect. At this equilibrium, what is the market price? What would be the equilibrium number of kidneys people would buy?

# ACTIVITY 7.1 (continued)
# A MARKET IN KIDNEYS

**7.** How has the rise in price affected the behavior of suppliers? To answer, compare the new equilibrium quantity with your answer to Question 1. Can you make any generalizations about the people who might sell a kidney at the equilibrium price but would not donate a kidney when the price is $0?

**8.** How has the rise in price affected the behavior of consumers (patients)? To answer, compare the new equilibrium quantity with your answer to Question 3. Can you make any generalizations about the people who might demand a kidney when the price is $0 but who will not buy one when the price reaches equilibrium?

**9.** According to the graph, how many kidney transplants would occur each year at the new equilibrium price? How much of a shortage exists at this price?

**10.** Assuming all other factors are constant, would a free market for kidneys result in more or fewer kidney-related deaths each year?

## ACTIVITY 7.1 (continued)
## A MARKET IN KIDNEYS

**11.** Would a free market in kidneys be fair to poor people? Argue both sides of this issue.

**12.** If the legal price of kidneys is very high, does this pose a risk to public safety: Is there an incentive for organ theft?

**13.** Do you think that either the supply or demand curve might shift if the government instituted a legal market for kidneys? If so, which curve would shift and in which direction?

**14.** Assume there was a successful campaign to encourage more donations of kidneys. How would this campaign shift the supply curve? How would this campaign affect the equilibrium price and quantity of kidneys? What would happen to the shortage of kidneys?

**15.** Is the graph for a market in kidneys realistic? Why?

# ACTIVITY 7.2
# THE ETHICS OF A LEGAL MARKET IN KIDNEYS

Is it desirable to buy and sell kidneys? To answer this question, you must apply ethical reasoning and economic analysis. This requires some understanding of ethical theories, along with the main arguments for and against them.

The purpose of ethics is to guide action. Every human action involves 1) an agent who performs 2) some action that has 3) particular consequences:

Agent   ▶   Action   ▶   Consequences

Each of the three main types of ethical theories focuses on a different part of this sequence. Starting with the last item first, these are the theories:

## OUTCOMES-BASED ETHICS (RIGHT CONSEQUENCES)

According to outcomes-based ethics, the best action is the one that produces the best consequences. It's the results that truly matter. The idea is first to define what is most valuable and then act to maximize this valuable outcome.

Modern economic welfare theory is outcomes-based. The most highly valued goal is the capacity to satisfy consumer preferences. According to this theory, we would evaluate the market for kidneys on the basis of whether the market increases the availability of these organs to the consumers who are most willing and able to buy them, reducing or eliminating the waiting list for kidney transplants.

Not all outcomes-based ethicists would agree that satisfying consumer preferences is the main goal. Some may give higher priority to outcomes that they believe are fair or that achieve some other objective such as public safety.

## DUTY-BASED ETHICS (RIGHT ACTION)

Duty-based ethics focuses on a set of ethical principles, duties or rules to guide action or process. Basic ethical duties or rights are "absolute" or "unalienable" (as in the U.S. Declaration of Independence) and should be respected regardless of other considerations. For example, it is never ethical to murder someone, even if this outcome would produce the greatest happiness for the rest of society.

# ACTIVITY 7.2 (continued)
# THE ETHICS OF A LEGAL MARKET IN KIDNEYS

The Ten Commandments are an example of religious ethical rules. Many religious traditions regard the human body as sacred and inviolate. Would it defile religious law to regard the body as a commodity that can be bought and sold? Would organ sales open the door to the sale of children or to prostitution?

## VIRTUE-BASED ETHICS (RIGHT AGENT)

Virtue-based ethics starts with the intentions of agents who are contemplating taking some action. Virtues are the personal qualities that enable us to do the things that good people do. Good people have ideal character traits that include honesty, integrity, courage, concern for others and loyalty.

Would a virtuous person buy and sell human organs? Exemplars such as Mother Teresa, Martin Luther King Jr. and Abraham Lincoln set admirable examples for some virtue ethicists. The "WWJD" printed on T-shirts and billboards means "What would Jesus do?" On a more modest level, our model might be "What would our mother or father do?"

# ACTIVITY 7.2 (continued)
# THE ETHICS OF A LEGAL MARKET IN KIDNEYS

**Questions**

**1.** What are the advantages and disadvantages of an ethical theory that focuses on satisfying consumer preferences in a market?

**2.** What are the advantages and disadvantages of using absolute ethical rules to determine public policy for kidneys?

**3.** How would you describe the ideal human character? How might your description affect your analysis of buying and selling kidneys?

**4.** In considering the buying and selling of kidneys, which ethical approach influences you most? Why?

# ACTIVITY 7.3
# WHICH POLICY DO YOU FAVOR?

**Directions:** The previous Activities have provided you with an economic and ethical basis for evaluating kidney-transplant policies. Now it is time for you to be the policy maker. Read the following information and then decide which policy you support. Be ready to justify your decision. Which policy saves the most lives? Which conforms most closely to the ethical framework you find most acceptable?

## OPTION 1: THE CURRENT SYSTEM

A national law makes it illegal to sell human organs. Anyone who sells a kidney faces jail, fines or both. People may donate kidneys, however, and doctors distribute donated kidneys on the basis of need. Some of the factors they consider in allocating kidneys are the patient's age and medical condition, how long the patient has been on a waiting list and whether the donor is in the local area.

Under this system, there is a shortage of kidneys, and many people are on a waiting list for years. During this time they receive costly dialysis treatment, and many people die.

## OPTION 2: AN OPEN MARKET

Create an open market in kidneys. People may sell their kidneys on the market for the highest price they can get. They may sell and deliver a kidney while they are still alive, or they may sell for delivery after they die. Brokerage firms match buyers and sellers. People could even sell kidneys on eBay. Recipients would pay for the kidney the same way they pay for other medical care: with their own funds or through insurance, government programs and charity.

# ACTIVITY 7.3 (continued)
# WHICH POLICY DO YOU FAVOR?

## OPTION 3: A REGULATED MARKET

Create a market in which anyone may sell a kidney, but only authorized institutions such as hospitals may legally buy. This option reduces the possibility of acquiring kidneys through involuntary means such as theft or murder. The institutions would allocate the kidneys on a basis similar to the way kidneys are allocated today using age, medical need or time spent on a waiting list. Recipients would pay for the kidneys with private funds, insurance, government assistance and charity.

## OPTION 4: A COMMUNITARIAN APPROACH

This approach uses nonmarket mechanisms to increase the supply in several ways.

A marketing campaign would increase people's awareness of the issue and alter their preferences for organ donation through moral persuasion. The slogan for a national television campaign might be "Friends don't let friends waste the gift of life." This is not an appeal to altruism but to people's sense of moral obligation and duty.

A more authoritarian policy would legally mandate that when people die, all their organs will be donated unless they indicate otherwise. People who don't want to donate must take the extra step to note this in advance on their driver's license. Today people must agree in advance for their organs to be donated.

# Lesson 8 — Is Efficiency an Ethical Concept?

*The students play the role of a doctor facing a critical shortage of life-saving serum and learn that any definition of efficiency requires judgments about what most improves society's welfare.*

## OVERVIEW

### Economics

In a world of scarcity, eliminating waste creates new possibilities — for saving more lives, feeding more families and overcoming real material limitations. So economists are justly concerned with efficiency. As this lesson shows, however, economists define efficiency in relation to society's goals. Whether they realize it or not, economists operate within an ethical framework when they evaluate economic efficiency.

### Ethics

Welfare economics is the branch of economics that studies economic institutions, individual actions and public policies. Every public-policy analysis involves a judgment about what welfare is and how welfare can be enhanced. By understanding the ethical judgments required to define and measure efficiency, economists can better understand and address real-world public-policy problems.

## LESSON DESCRIPTION

In this lesson the students discover how goals and value judgments affect decisions about efficiency and welfare. They also learn how economists measure efficiency. First, the students discuss the concepts of positive economics, normative economics, productive efficiency and allocative efficiency. Then they play the role of a doctor facing a critical shortage of life-saving serum and discuss the role of efficiency in allocating this serum. They read an Activity and answer questions about how economists approach the issues of efficiency and welfare. Returning to the case of the doctor, the students see how economists analyze efficiency and welfare.

## CONCEPTS

Allocative efficiency
Consumer welfare
Incentives
Normative economics
Positive economics
Productive efficiency
Welfare economics

## CONTENT STANDARDS

3. Different methods can be used to allocate goods and services. People, acting individually or collectively through government, must choose which methods to use to allocate different kinds of goods and services.

4. People respond predictably to positive and negative incentives.

8. Prices send signals and provide incentives to buyers and sellers. When supply or demand changes, market prices adjust, affecting incentives.

9. Competition among sellers lowers costs and prices, and encourages producers to produce more of what consumers are will-

ing and able to buy. Competition among buyers increases prices and allocates goods and services to those people who are willing and able to pay the most for them.

## OBJECTIVES

The students will:

1. Distinguish between normative and positive economics, and see how both types of analysis are necessary for debating public-policy issues.

2. Describe how economists define welfare and efficiency.

3. Explain why economic efficiency sometimes conflicts with other objectives of society.

4. Evaluate alternative conceptions of efficiency and welfare.

## TIME REQUIRED

45 minutes

## MATERIALS

1. Visuals 8.1 and 8.2

2. One copy of Activities 8.1 and 8.2 for each student

## PROCEDURE

1. Tell the class that the purpose of this lesson is to learn how economists measure the performance of the microeconomy in terms of efficiency. As part of the activity, they will evaluate the efficiency of different allocations of health care.

2. Display Visual 8.1 and review the definitions of positive economics (facts) and normative economics (values). Tell the class that economists must often analyze public-policy proposals. To make a policy recommendation, they must collect facts (positive economics) and weigh the importance of different goals (normative economics).

3. Tell the students that efficiency means being effective at achieving an objective. Economists must always define efficiency in relation to the goals of society. For example, a doctor in a hospital has to make life-and-death decisions. We can measure the doctor's efficiency in several different ways — for example, by the number of lives the doctor has saved.

4. Divide the students into small groups, and give each student a copy of Activity 8.1. Ask the students to work in their group to answer the questions. Then discuss the answers with the class.

   **Question 1:** How many lives could you save if you gave all the serum to patients with Disease A? *You have 10 doses of serum, and each patient with Disease A can be cured with one dose. Therefore, you could save 10 lives if you gave all the serum to Disease A patients.*

   **Question 2:** How many lives could you save if you gave all the serum to patients with Disease B? *Each Disease B patient requires two doses of serum to be cured. Therefore, with only 10 doses of serum, you could, at most, save five lives. You wouldn't save any lives if you divided the serum equally among the Disease B patients, since each patient would get only one dose and each would die.*

   **Question 3:** Which allocation option is the most efficient at saving lives in this situation? *Giving the serum to Disease A patients would save twice as many lives as giving it to Disease B patients. Allocating serum to Disease A patients is the most efficient option.*

   **Question 4:** Assuming you have no additional information, which option would you use to allocate the serum and why? *If a doctor's goal is to save the most lives at this moment, the doctor would give all the serum to patients with Disease A and none to patients with Disease B.*

   **Question 5:** Suppose you learn that

patients with Disease B are all young children and patients with Disease A are all more than 80 years old. Would this change your serum allocation, and if so, why? *Answers will vary, but many students would now be inclined to save as many children as possible, because the number of years each child has to live exceeds the likely survival years of an elderly person. This approach is called saving the most "life-years extended."*

**Question 6:** In light of your answers to Questions 4 and 5, is being efficient at saving the most lives today the only value society should be concerned with? *Society has other concerns in addition to saving specific lives today. For example, society has a strong concern for the preservation and reproduction of its members, which would place greater weight on saving the lives of children. Also, society is often concerned with treating patients fairly. In addition, society may be concerned about the incentives that different allocation methods create. Lives lost today must be weighed against lives potentially lost in the future.*

**Question 7:** Which of the questions above can you answer using positive economics and which involve normative economics? Explain your answer. *Questions 1, 2 and 3 can be answered by facts alone and are thus positive. Question 4 requires a normative judgment that saving the most lives today is the highest goal, and therefore the allocation options should be judged on that basis. Questions 5 and 6 are also normative because they require judgments about what society's goals ought to be.*

5.  Ask the students what they learned from this role-play experience. *The key point to bring out is that people must know the objective or goal before they know how to act.*

6.  Use Visual 8.2 to highlight the way economists currently define welfare and efficiency. Society has many possible goals that provide for the general welfare. These include preserving freedom, maintaining national security, improving standards of living and providing opportunities for all citizens. In an economic context, we can define consumer welfare more precisely: It is the ability of an economy to satisfy individual consumer preferences.

    *Allocative efficiency* means that consumers are able to obtain the goods and services that best satisfy their individual preferences, given their income constraints. To help the students understand the importance of this concept, ask: "If a dictator were to require everyone to buy only classical music, would this satisfy individual consumer preferences? Is the dictator concerned about consumer welfare?" Most command economies such as communism take away the freedoms of consumers to make their own choices about what to buy.

7.  Give each student a copy of Activity 8.2. This activity describes how economists define efficiency in relation to society's goals. Give the students time to read the activity and work in small groups to answer the questions. Begin the class discussion with Questions 1, 2 and 3.

    **Question 1:** Anthony drove to New York's Kennedy Airport in record time. However, his plane was leaving from a different airport — in Newark, N.J. Was Anthony's driving efficient? *No. Since his goal was to fly out of Newark, driving to Kennedy Airport in New York was not efficient, regardless of how quickly he got there. This answer highlights the importance of knowing the goal before trying to measure efficiency.*

    **Question 2:** Why should you define a goal before you measure efficiency? *Being efficient means achieving some objective in the best possible manner. So, you should first define the objective or goal.*

**Question 3:** Are the definitions of welfare and efficiency part of positive or normative economics? *Choosing one welfare goal among competing goals requires us to decide what is most important. Doing so involves a consideration of values, not facts. Because we must choose a welfare goal before defining efficiency, both concepts relate to normative economics.*

8. Tell the students that any discussion about what improves the welfare of society will be controversial because people don't necessarily agree on the most important goals of society. Economists themselves have had diverging viewpoints historically. As a result, the way economists define welfare and efficiency has changed over time.

9. Discuss the answers to Questions 4 through 11 with the class.

    **Question 4:** How do consumers express their preferences in the marketplace? *In a market system, consumers express their preferences by spending money in ways that send profit or loss signals to producers. In competitive markets, businesses make profits by trying to satisfy consumer preferences.*

    **Question 5:** If Manuel, who loves rock music, had received an inheritance instead of Mary, how might the outcome in terms of the concert tickets have changed? Would this change be allocatively efficient? *Manuel may have ended up with the concert tickets instead of Mary. This would have been allocatively efficient because Manuel now has the income with which to express his preferences (but Mary does not). Accordingly, there will be a different allocatively efficient outcome for each different distribution of income.*

    **Question 6:** If Bill has no income, how are his preferences accounted for in the market? *The preferences of consumers who have no income (or choose not to spend it) are not counted in a market. In practice, however, even people with*

*no income usually have some spending power because of gifts or social programs such as Social Security.*

**Question 7:** Suppose that Disease A patients have low incomes and Disease B patients have high incomes. Which option for allocating serum would be most efficient in terms of satisfying individual consumer preferences in the market? *Assuming no market failures, allocative efficiency is achieved when consumers get to buy what they want within the limits of their incomes, and their preferences are satisfied. People with higher incomes will bid up the price of the serum. A rise in price serves to ration the scarce serum to people who are most willing and able to buy. Patients with Disease B will get all the serum in this case. The price allocation mechanism is efficient if the goal is satisfying consumer preferences.*

**Question 8:** How many lives are saved in the short run using the market-allocation approach? *In the short run, only five Disease B patients — those with the greatest willingness and ability to pay — are saved. Note that this outcome may seem paradoxical because the market-efficient approach results in fewer lives saved. Tell the students that this paradox will be resolved in Question 9 by considering the long-run situation.*

**Question 9:** In this example, what are the advantages and disadvantages of the market approach to drug allocation? *One disadvantage of the market approach in this example is that more patients would die in the short run if Disease B patients buy all the serum. Satisfying the preferences of well-off patients may seem unfair to poor patients. But economists are interested in how incentives alter behavior in the long run. Relying on markets and profits may attract more resources into research and development of new drugs and innovative treatments,* *thereby creating long-run dynamic efficiency gains. Accounting for these long-run supply effects, the market approach has the potential to save more lives in the long run. Market supporters also note that any nonmarket allocation system — for example, price controls, rationing and favoritism — would require government force. What government entity will decide who gets the serum? The resulting loss of personal freedom and the destruction of incentives needed for production would produce high costs for any alternative system.*

**Question 10:** In considering how health care is provided, what values besides allocative efficiency are important to society? *Public policy is based on consideration of a broad mix of goals and values in addition to allocative efficiency. These goals include public safety (saving the most lives), fairness, freedom, national security, human rights and income distribution. When these goals conflict, people must rank them in order to reach a decision. Economists have long noted the conflict between efficiency and equity concerns.*

**Question 11:** Would government decisions about health-care allocation be more fair than market decisions? *The students' answers may vary, and this question can provoke some lively discussion.*

*If government allocated health care by using a lottery, for example, this might benefit some poor consumers who otherwise might not be able to pay. But a lottery would also mean that a patient who is less sick than another patient might win the treatment. The students could see this as unfair, since someone in greater need of care goes without.*

*If government allocated health care using some degree of favoritism — based, say, on the severity of illness — the sickest patients would get treatment first. But patients then have an incentive to lie to their doctors about*

*the severity of their illnesses or even to bribe doctors to provide a more severe diagnosis. Medical-care favoritism might be biased toward patients who wield the greatest power or have the strongest political connections. Thus there is no guarantee that government allocations would go to people in greatest need.*

*This brief analysis suggests that there is no easy answer about which allocation system is most fair. The market solution, by virtue of providing proper incentives, creates conditions in which consumer welfare can be maximized. Some consider this more fair than other allocation mechanisms since each consumer's dollar is weighted equally, without favoritism.*

## CLOSURE

10. Ask the students to consider how they might allocate scarce serum in the hospital. What values would be most important to them in reaching their decision? *Answers will vary. Many students will find it highly objectionable to allow the market to make life-and-death decisions, particularly in this case since more patients might die in the short run. It is important for the students to realize that the visible effects in the short run are not the only effects. An economic perspective would analyze long-run consequences for society as well.*

*In the long run, the market approach may save many more lives. Values of efficiency come into conflict with other values such as perceived fairness and basic human rights. While it may be easy for the students to mandate nonmarket allocations in this case, ask them to consider whether government intervention would be desirable in other areas such as electricity, housing and food. The loss of individual freedom and the loss of incentives for production and innovation are large concerns for society.*

**The bottom line:** Efficiency must always be defined in relation to the goals of society. Achieving such efficiency may conflict with other values of society. By understanding the judgments required to define welfare and efficiency, economists can better understand real-world public-policy problems.

## ASSESSMENT

### Multiple-Choice Questions

8.1 What welfare goal is allocative efficiency based on?
    *A. The satisfaction of individual consumer preferences*
    B. The greatest happiness for the poorest members of society
    C. Saving the most lives
    D. Being fair to all citizens

8.2 Joan received a birthday gift of an expensive pink sweater. She hates pink and would prefer to return the sweater to the store and use the money for dinner and a movie. From Joan's perspective, the current allocation of goods is
    A. efficient because people should treasure the gifts they receive.
    B. efficient because Joan hasn't yet returned the sweater.
    C. inefficient because the gift was from a family member.
    *D. inefficient because it doesn't satisfy Joan's preferences.*

8.3 An economic policy could create economic efficiency but might not be fair. To resolve this problem requires the use of
    A. aggregate economics.
    *B. normative economics.*
    C. inflation economics.
    D. positive economics.

### Essay Questions

8.1 What do modern economists mean by welfare and allocative efficiency? How do economists apply these concepts to public-policy analysis? What problems exist with the use of these concepts? *Economists define welfare as "the satisfaction of consumer preferences." Allocative efficiency means the economy is producing the right mix of goods and services, and no voluntary trade is possible that would make one person better and leave no one else worse off. The economic definition of efficiency may conflict with other definitions of efficiency such as saving the most lives. Other values besides welfare and efficiency arise in public-policy deliberations: fairness, freedom and public safety, for example.*

8.2 There are 10 people and space for only five in a life raft. How would you decide which people get a place on the raft? What solution to this problem would economists consider allocatively efficient? What other values besides efficiency are important in analyzing this situation? *All definitions of welfare and efficiency involve normative judgments about what is most important to society. Allocative efficiency means allowing consumers to buy goods and services that satisfy their preferences. Hence, the highest bidders could satisfy their preferences by bidding for a spot on the life raft. This could be considered fair if the income distribution in society is considered fair. However, the efficient approach comes into conflict with other social values, which include fairness, basic equality of all and human dignity. In deciding public-policy issues, society considers not only efficiency but also a host of other values.*

## GOING FURTHER

**Health Data and Costs:** The debate about
whether to pay for medical care with private
or public financing is contentious precisely
because of the issues raised in this lesson. The
United States relies more heavily on market
forces to allocate health care than other industrialized countries. Hence, about 41 million
Americans do not have any health-insurance
coverage, although most still have some access
to care. Health expenditures per capita are
far higher in the United States than in other
industrialized countries, even though some
health indicators lag. To review comparative
health indicators and expenditures, see Gerard
F. Anderson, Varduhi Petrosyan and Peter S.
Hussey, "Multinational Comparisons of Health
Systems Data, 2002," The Commonwealth
Fund, October 2002, available online at
http://www.cmwf.org/usr_doc/Anderson_
healthpop_multi99_354.pdf

**Market-Based Health Care:** For a general
overview of the pros and cons of market-based
health care, go to
http://www.oheschools.org/index.html

**Innovation and Market-Based Health
Care:** A key argument for the support of
market-based health care is that it produces
dynamic gains in health-care quality through
innovation. For support of the market view, see
the list of online publications at
http://www.amatecon.com/

**Health-Care Rationing in the Movies:**
The movie *John Q* (2002) provides a potent
example of medical-care rationing to the unin-
sured or underinsured. The movie is generally
antimarket, but it does illustrate the short-run
versus long-run issues raised in Activity 8.2.

# VISUAL 8.1
# POSITIVE VERSUS NORMATIVE ECONOMICS

**POSITIVE ECONOMICS** involves statements of fact.

**Fact:** If cigarettes are taxed, fewer teenagers will be able to afford to buy cigarettes.

**NORMATIVE ECONOMICS** involves judgments of value.

**Judgment:** Parents should discourage teenagers from smoking.

**PUBLIC POLICY** involves both positive and normative analyses.

**Fact and Judgment:** Public-policy recommendations involve the desire to achieve the normative goal (fewer teenagers who smoke) and a positive model (facts) that predicts how a tax might achieve the desired goal.

VISUAL 8.2
WHAT IS EFFICIENCY?

## 1. DEFINING THE GOAL: What is most important?

Society has many possible goals. These include preserving freedom, maintaining national security, improving standards of living and providing opportunities for all citizens. In addition, economists often focus specifically on the goal of enhancing "welfare."

*Consumer welfare* means the ability of an economy to satisfy individual consumer preferences.

## 2. MEASURING SUCCESS: How do we know we have achieved the goal of enhancing consumer welfare?

*Allocative efficiency* means that consumers are able to obtain the goods and services that best satisfy their individual preferences, given their income constraints.

# ACTIVITY 8.1
# SOLVING A PUBLIC-HEALTH PROBLEM

You are a doctor who runs a hospital in an isolated rural area. You have 20 very sick patients: 10 patients have Disease A and 10 patients have Disease B. All the patients will die unless they quickly receive the correct dose of life-saving serum.
  • Each patient with Disease A needs one dose of serum to be cured.
  • Each patient with Disease B needs two doses of serum to be cured.
**Problem:** You have only 10 doses of serum, and you don't have time to get more.

**Questions**

**1.** How many lives could you save if you gave all the serum to patients with Disease A?

**2.** How many lives could you save if you gave all the serum to patients with Disease B?

**3.** Which allocation option is the most efficient at saving lives in this situation?

# ACTIVITY 8.1 (continued)
# SOLVING A PUBLIC-HEALTH PROBLEM

**4.** Assuming you have no additional information, which option would you use to allocate the serum and why?

**5.** Suppose you learn that patients with Disease B are all young children and patients with Disease A are all more than 80 years old. Would this change your serum allocation, and if so, why?

**6.** In light of your answers to Questions 4 and 5, is being efficient at saving the most lives today the only value society should be concerned with?

**7.** Which of the questions above can you answer using positive economics and which involve normative economics? Explain your answer.

## ACTIVITY 8.2
## WELFARE, EFFICIENCY AND ETHICS

**Directions:** Read the following information, and work in small groups to answer the questions.

How should economists measure efficiency? And is greater efficiency always a good thing?

Miles per gallon (MPG) measures the efficiency of a vehicle's engine in terms of how many miles you can drive on one gallon of gas (outputs produced per inputs used).

*Productive efficiency* means producing the most output possible using the fewest input of resources.

Productive efficiency is scientific and objective. But this doesn't mean a higher MPG is always the best outcome. Getting more miles per gallon could be good, assuming everything else is constant. Sometimes it is possible to achieve higher mileage just by making sure the air pressure in the tires is correct. But in real life it is rarely possible to get something for nothing. Getting more miles per gallon might require auto manufacturers to make the car lighter. A lighter car might not be as safe, so having a more efficient engine might reduce efficiency in something you value even more: saving your life.

We need to know which goal is most important. Because society has competing goals, deciding what is efficient requires choosing the goal that most improves the welfare of society. This requires a value judgment rather than facts alone.

### Welfare And Efficiency

Welfare concerns the question "what makes society better off?" Any definition of welfare is open to debate and could change over time. One economic definition of welfare isn't something tangible like a life saved or miles per gallon. Instead, the goal of an economy is to satisfy the preferences of individual consumers. With this goal in mind:

*Allocative efficiency* is achieved when individuals are able to obtain the goods and services that best satisfy their preferences.

# ACTIVITY 8.2 (continued)
# WELFARE, EFFICIENCY AND ETHICS

Suppose Manuel has a pair of rock-concert tickets that he values at $200, but Mary, a wealthy heiress, is willing and able to buy them for $1,000. Is society's welfare maximized by the current allocation?

No. The current allocation of tickets does not reflect consumer preferences. Manuel has the tickets, but Mary values them more. This outcome is inefficient because it doesn't maximize the welfare of society.

How can the economy be made more efficient? Manuel and Mary can improve their welfares through voluntary trade. If Manuel is permitted to sell the tickets to Mary, he receives $1,000, which he values more than the tickets. Mary gets the tickets, which she values more than the $1,000. The welfare of society is improved through trade. Economists would say the economy is allocatively efficient only after all voluntary trades between individuals have been allowed. After this point, it is impossible to make one person better off without making another person worse off.

Economists infer that Manuel and Mary are better off after trading (more preferences satisfied) by observing their actions. In a marketplace, consumers reveal their preferences (and their buying power) when they engage in market activity.

Competitive markets do a reasonable job of achieving allocative efficiency because businesses have a profit incentive to make products that consumers want and to get these products to the consumers who desire them the most. As noted, however, the conclusion that markets serve the needs of society is the result of science (involving theories of supply and demand) and important value judgments about the desired goals of an economy.

### Reconsidering Lives Saved

Let's return to the case of the hospital in Activity 8.1. The hospital has 20 patients who will die without the life-saving serum, but only 10 doses of the serum are available today. To save the most lives today, we discovered that a doctor would administer all of the serum to patients with Disease A. We have already shown that if the goal is different — to save the most lives of children

# ACTIVITY 8.2 (continued)
# WELFARE, EFFICIENCY AND ETHICS

— the doctor might efficiently choose to allocate the serum differently by giving it to half of the children with Disease B.

Allowing the serum to be sold in the marketplace would also result in a different outcome. Since consumer preferences are expressed through market activity, welfare is measured by what consumers are willing and able to pay for life-saving serum. The allocatively efficient outcome is achieved when patients can bid for the scarce serum. Patients who are willing and able to pay the most would get the serum (their preferences would be satisfied).

With a market approach there is no guarantee that only Disease A patients would get the serum, so this approach isn't likely to save the most lives in this short-run scenario.

## The Long Run

The previous section provides insight into some of the controversies about the U.S. health-care system. Millions of poor people don't have the spending power to buy health care or health insurance. Consequently, critics note that although the United States spends a larger share of its GDP on health care, it lags other industrial countries in several basic indicators of health achievement, especially for the poor. Because of this, some people say the market approach to allocation is cruel and unfair. These people believe all individuals have the same right to treatment, and ability to pay shouldn't be a factor in health-care allocation. Other people might criticize the market approach, saying it justifies the treatment of patients as commodities. For many people, there are some decisions about health that shouldn't be left to the market.

Supporters of the market reply that the reason the United States lags in some health indicators is complex and may have more to do with lifestyle and genetics than health policy. They also note that poor patients are still able to receive life-saving treatment through government programs and by showing up at emergency rooms where certain types of care are provided regardless of the patient's ability to pay. In short, patients still have health coverage even if they don't have health insurance.

# ACTIVITY 8.2 (continued)
# WELFARE, EFFICIENCY AND ETHICS

Most importantly, the short run may be the wrong time period of analysis. Economists believe that a long-run perspective is often more useful at illustrating the real-world trade-offs that society must face. In particular, economists concern themselves with the invisible and often unintended consequences of policies whose effects may appear only in the long run.

To illustrate, let's go forward in time five years to see how patients are faring under two different allocation systems.

Suppose that medicines were allocated in a marketplace, and consumers were bidding up serum prices. Economists reason that as prices rise, businesses have an economic incentive to manufacture more serum. Thus, in the long run, the expansion of existing firms and the entry of new firms could greatly increase the quantity of medicines available. These conditions could also spur innovation and the discovery of new and better medicines. The result: In the long run, the market-allocation approach might save more lives.

Economists can't know this outcome in advance, so they must have faith in the way markets work. Economists are quick to note that this desirable outcome relies on competition, or at least the threat of competition, which may not exist in some health-care markets. Historical evidence indicates that the United States is far ahead of other countries in terms of new medical innovations.

By contrast, allocating goods without concern for price, cost or profit in the short run might save more lives today (the visible effect) but cost more lives in the long run (the invisible effect). Without profits, firms would leave the industry and innovation would stagnate. Patients might have to wait a long time for critical supplies. In other words, the way medicines are allocated in the short run could affect the availability and quality of medicines in the long run. Thinking like an economist means trying to discern the invisible long-run effects.

## ACTIVITY 8.2 (continued)
## WELFARE, EFFICIENCY AND ETHICS

### Questions

**1.** Anthony drove to New York's Kennedy Airport in record time. However, his plane was leaving from a different airport — in Newark, N.J. Was Anthony's driving efficient?

**2.** Why should you define a goal before you measure efficiency?

**3.** Are the definitions of welfare and efficiency part of positive or normative economics?

**4.** How do consumers express their preferences in the marketplace?

**5.** If Manuel, who loves rock music, had received an inheritance instead of Mary, how might the outcome in terms of the concert tickets have changed? Would this change be allocatively efficient?

# ACTIVITY 8.2 (continued)
# WELFARE, EFFICIENCY AND ETHICS

**6.** If Bill has no income, how are his preferences accounted for in the market?

**7.** Suppose that Disease A patients have low incomes and Disease B patients have high incomes. Which option for allocating serum would be most efficient in terms of satisfying individual consumer preferences in the market?

**8.** How many lives are saved in the short run using the market-allocation approach?

**9.** In this example, what are the advantages and disadvantages of the market approach to drug allocation?

**10.** In considering how health care is provided, what values besides allocative efficiency are important to society?

**11.** Would government decisions about health-care allocation be more fair than market decisions?

# Lesson 9 – Do Businesses Have A Social Responsibility?

*The students debate whether a business best serves society's interests by maximizing profits or by pursuing policies it believes promote social justice, the environment and other causes.*

## OVERVIEW

### Economics
Many workers are employees of companies. These workers agree to do what the companies' owners tell them to do. In return, the companies pay the employees a wage or salary. This relationship, or contract, is an example of a principal-agent agreement: The company is the principal and the worker is the agent. The principal-agent agreement is the most common employment contract in capitalist countries. It is the basis of the economic model for businesses, most of which consider their sole purpose to be maximizing profits for owners. In a publicly traded company, the owners are the company's shareholders.

### Ethics
Advocates of corporate social responsibility argue that profit is essential to a business's well-being and continued existence, but profit should not entirely define the business's purpose. These advocates believe the principal-agent agreement also has a trust or fiduciary aspect that includes a set of expectations related to honesty, loyalty, obedience and the full disclosure of relevant facts. Workers have a fiduciary duty to their employer, for example, to obey the firm's rules. A company has a fiduciary duty to its shareholders to report financial data honestly. But advocates of corporate social responsibility believe that a firm's fiduciary duty extends beyond its shareholders to other stakeholders: employees, suppliers, customers and the community.

## LESSON DESCRIPTION

The students read two viewpoints on the social responsibility of business: Milton Friedman, a Nobel laureate in economics, argues that businesses best fulfill their social responsibilities to society by focusing on increased profits. John Mackey, founder of Whole Foods Market, believes that a business's social responsibility goes beyond maximizing profits. The students evaluate these arguments and then decide whose opinion they support.

## CONCEPTS

Fiduciary duty
Principal-agent agreement
Profit
Shareholder
Social responsibility of business
Stakeholder

## CONTENT STANDARDS

10. Institutions evolve in market economies to help individuals and groups accomplish their goals. Banks, labor unions, corporations, legal systems, and not-for-profit organizations are examples of important institutions. A different kind of institution, clearly defined and well enforced property rights, is essential to a market economy.

14. Entrepreneurs are people who take the risks of organizing productive resources to make goods and services. Profit is an important incentive that leads entrepreneurs to accept the risks of business failure.

## OBJECTIVES

The students will:

1. Describe the principal-agent agreement that governs most employment.

2. Compare and contrast two views on the social responsibility of business.

3. Analyze the reasoning behind different views on social responsibility of business.

## TIME REQUIRED

60 minutes

## MATERIALS

1. Visuals 9.1 and 9.2

2. One copy of Activity 9.1 for each student

3. Five sheets of paper with "1" written on one, "2" on another, "3" on another, "4" on another and "5" on another.

## PROCEDURE

1. Tell the students they are going to investigate whether businesses have a social responsibility beyond making *profits* for the company owners, or *shareholders*. Some people believe businesses best serve society by increasing profits — as long as they adhere to the laws and ethical customs of society. Others believe businesses have an obligation beyond maximizing profits: to improve the economic and social lives of the communities in which they operate.

2. Give each student a copy of Activity 9.1. Tell the students that the authors they are going to read are notable figures in the debate about corporate social responsibility. Milton Friedman won the 1976 Nobel Prize in economic sciences. John Mackey is the founder of Whole Foods Market, a business that has billions of dollars of sales each year. Have the students read the articles and write the answers to the questions. To save time, you may want to assign the reading as homework.

3. Discuss the answers to the questions in Activity 9.1. Do not expect the students' answers to be as complete as the answers below. However, you can use some of the points in these answers to move the discussion along.

**Question 1:** According to Milton Friedman, what is the responsibility of corporate executives? *To conduct the business in accordance with owners' (shareholders') desires, which generally will be to make as much money as possible without violating society's basic rules and ethical customs*

**Question 2:** Beyond making a profit, what ethical responsibilities does Friedman say businesses have to society in general? *Friedman believes businesses have no ethical responsibilities to society in general except to follow the rules society expects businesses to follow. Only people can be ethical. People who work for a business owe general ethical duties to society such as being honest with customers and suppliers. However, it is only as a private person, not as an employee, that one has obligations to family, clubs and country.*

**Question 3:** Does Friedman's emphasis on maximizing corporate profits mean that he is not concerned with the welfare of society? *No. The search for greater profits causes corporations to reallocate resources from low-value products to high-value products. If a product is earning a large profit, this signals to producers that consumers desire more of it and encourages producers to increase output and satisfy this demand. Profits also create incentives for firms to search for new products, technologies and inventions. Profits are an incentive to produce more efficiently. Competitive markets are dynamic. They meet society's need for efficiency, growth and freedom. Corporate executives benefit society more by responding to market signals than by indulging their own causes with shareholders' money.*

**Question 4:** Why does Friedman believe a corporate executive should be socially responsible as an individual but not in his or her corporate role? *The executive is an agent of the business owner and therefore is responsible only to the goals of the owner. This is the principal-agent system. The owner is the principal, and the executive is the agent. As an individual, the corporate executive has many responsibilities, but in these cases the executive acts as a principal, not an agent.*

**Question 5:** What is the difference between a shareholder and a stakeholder? *A shareholder is a person or group that owns stock in a company. This gives the shareholder part ownership of the company. A stakeholder is anyone who is affected by the company. This goes beyond shareholders to include workers, customers, suppliers and the wider community in which the company operates.*

**Question 6:** Who are the stakeholders in John Mackey's conception of the corporation? What ethical duties does the corporation owe to each stakeholder? *Mackey identifies his stakeholders but does not clearly address what Whole Foods owes them, since he says this will change over time. Ask the students to guess what Mackey believes his company would owe each of these stakeholders:*

*Customers — honesty, service, reasonable price*

*Team members (employees) — honesty, reward, recognition*

*Shareholders — return on capital, profits, psychic income*

*Suppliers — honesty, loyalty, stable business relationship with a fair financial reward*

*Communities — giving 5 percent of profits to community causes*

*Environment — stewardship*

**Question 7:** What motives besides money does Mackey argue are important in understanding human nature? How might these motives be relevant in running a business? *Mackey focuses on Adam Smith's notion of moral sentiments that arise from mutual sympathy. Moral sentiments exist for self-interest and also for generosity and justice. While modern economists have focused on sentiments of self-interest, Smith argues that people act out of all three instincts. If so, Mackey argues that tapping into instincts for generosity and justice can also act as powerful motivators, creating loyalty in workers, suppliers and other stakeholders.*

**Question 8:** Are Mackey's views on the social responsibility of business inconsistent with maximizing profits? Why? *Not necessarily. On the one hand, a company can have higher costs and lower profits by using revenue for socially responsible purposes. On the other hand, if consumers believe that Whole Foods is a good corporate citizen, they may be more willing to buy groceries at its stores, increasing business and profits.*

**Question 9:** Corporations have provided billions of dollars in aid to victims of Hurricane Katrina, the South Pacific tsunami and AIDS in Africa. In some cases, these contributions have been more effective than government aid. Would Friedman and Mackey support these types of donations? *Both men would want to understand the reasons behind the aid. They would approve if the donations generated good public relations and advertising for the firms and caused sales and profits to rise. But Mackey would approve even if the donations had no positive impact on the company's finances. He would say that corporations have an ethical duty to use some of their profits for the public good, as long as shareholders can question executives about such programs at the company's annual meetings.*

*Friedman would oppose philan-*

*thropic donations if a company's executives used them only to support their own personal causes or improve their personal reputations. He would say that the company should take the aid money and instead give it to shareholders by, say, raising the dividend on company stock. Then the shareholders could use the money to support their own favorite charities.*

4.  Display Visual 9.1 to summarize Friedman's and Mackey's different points of view. Make sure the students note that the key difference is in rows two and three. Friedman says only one stakeholder counts: the owners of company stock (shareholders). Mackey argues that the company owes an ethical duty to shareholders and to other stakeholders: customers, employees, suppliers, the community and the environment.

5.  Spread the five sheets of paper with numbers 1-5 written on them across the front of the room in the following order.

    | 1 | 2 | 3 | 4 | 5 |
    |---|---|---|---|---|
    | Mackey | | | | Friedman |
    | Social responsibility | | | | Profits only |

    Tell the students that No. 1 represents agreement with Mackey and his commitment to social responsibility. No. 5 represents Friedman and his commitment to profits. Ask the students to think about how much they agree with Friedman or Mackey. Say: "On a scale of 1 to 5, how much do you want firms to focus on making a profit for shareholders?" Have the students stand by the number they agree with. Students who agree with Friedman should stand by No. 5; those who agree with Mackey should stand by No. 1. Students who are in the middle should stand by No. 3.

6.  Tell the students: "Now pick a student you disagree with, have a five-minute discussion and prepare to report to the

class on your discussion. Then return to your seats." When all the students have returned to their seats, ask the pairs to briefly describe their discussion. Did either participant's opinion change? An alternative is to conduct a class discussion with the students standing by each number defending their position to the class.

## CLOSURE

7.  Display Visual 9.2. Read the quotation aloud, and then ask the students to answer the questions.

    **Question 1:** What do you think Smith means when he says that a merchant who strives only for his own gain unwittingly promotes the interests of society? What are society's interests, and how does the merchant promote them? *This quotation highlights the role that profit plays in allocating resources toward goods and services consumers desire. The merchant is seeking only profits, and this leads him to produce products that best satisfy consumer tastes and preferences for food, clothing, shelter and amusements.*

    **Question 2:** Whose position on the social responsibility of business does Smith's quotation support: Friedman's or Mackey's? *This quotation supports Friedman's view. However, other quotations from Smith support Mackey's view. Smith was concerned about social relations and particularly with ethical codes of conduct. Smith distinguished between legitimate self-interest and greed, which is excessive concern for self over others. (See Lesson 2.)*

    **Question 3:** Do you agree or disagree with this statement by Adam Smith? Why? *Answers will vary.*

**The bottom line:** Profits play a vital role in allocating resources into areas that serve society. No business can survive without profits. This does not mean that profits need to be the only goal of a company. Companies may have other goals that attract and inspire great workers, keep customers loyal and maintain reliable suppliers. These attributes can make a business very successful. Exactly how this is done is open to debate, and the articles in this lesson suggest two very different approaches.

## ASSESSMENT

### Multiple-Choice Questions

9.1 Which of the following is true of fiduciary duties?

    A. They are very unprofitable.

    *B. They bind employees to an expectation of honesty and loyalty to the employer.*

    C. Employees must adhere to them, but not employers.

    D. Employers must adhere to them, but not employees.

9.2 According to John Mackey,

    A. a company has an ethical duty only to its shareholders.

    B. achieving short-run profits is a company's principal goal.

    C. communities have obligations to employers.

    *D. businesses have obligations to community stakeholders.*

9.3 According to Milton Friedman,

    A. businesses should share their profits with customers and the community.

    B. neither individuals nor businesses have a social responsibility beyond making profits.

    *C. a company executive has a direct responsibility only to the company's owners (shareholders).*

    D. maximizing profits is not consistent with improving the welfare of society.

### Essay Questions

9.1 Compare and contrast the views of Milton Friedman and John Mackey on corporate social responsibility. Which view do you find more compelling and why? *Answers will vary. Friedman emphasizes the fiduciary duties of business managers to run the company to maximize profits for shareholders, who in Friedman's view are the only stakeholders. Mackey emphasizes the fiduciary duties of managers to many stakeholders, including workers, suppliers, customers and the community. Moreover, he supports the concept of a company as a beneficial social force beyond the profits it creates.*

9.2 Imagine that you are the CEO of a corporation. The mayor of the city where your corporate offices are located asks your corporation for a major donation to build a new community park and swimming pool. How would you respond? Explain your answer. *A weak answer would be based on whether or not the student liked the cause. A good answer should reflect the student's position on the social responsibility of business. From the Friedman perspective, the corporation should give the donation only if it increases the corporation's profits. From the Mackey perspective, making the donation would depend on whether it contributes to the common good of stakeholders such as consumers, employees and citizens of the city.*

## GOING FURTHER

### Stakeholder Theory

• For an introduction to stakeholder theory, see Edward R. Freeman, "Stakeholder Theory of the Modern Corporation," *Ethical Issues in Business: A Philosophical Approach*, eds. Thomas Donaldson and Patricia H. Werhane (Upper Saddle River, N.J.: Prentice Hall Inc., 2002).

• For additional background on stakeholder theory, see Robert Phillips, *Stakeholder Theory and Organizational Ethics* (San Francisco: Berrett-Koehler, 2003).

**Obliquity:** John Kay, former dean of the business school at Oxford University and a consultant to many companies, advocates an "oblique" approach to strategic management. He believes that a business can enhance its profit when it focuses on its intrinsic objectives (for example, quality, service and value) rather than directly on its extrinsic objective (profit). He believes this is particularly so within the complex environment of a multinational firm. For details, see *Culture and Prosperity: The truth about markets — Why some nations are rich but most remain poor* (New York: HarperBusiness, 2004).

**John Mackey's Blog:** Mackey has a blog on the Whole Foods Market Web site at http://www.wholefoods.com/blogs/jm/
 • To read the full text of Mackey's article in *Reason* magazine and responses from Milton Friedman and T.J. Rodgers, founder, president and chief executive officer of Cypress Semiconductor Corp., go here: http://www.wholefoods.com/blogs/jm/archives/2005/09/rethinking_the.html

**Mackey's Philosophy in Fiction:** For a fictional account of a business that follows John Mackey's approach, see Jonathan B. Wight, *Saving Adam Smith* (Upper Saddle River, N.J.: Prentice Hall Inc., 2002) — in particular the last third of the novel.

**Fortune 500 Companies and Corporate Philosophy:** Ask the students in advanced classes to research companies, some of which are listed below, that reportedly follow Mackey's approach and compare them with companies that do not.
 • McCormick & Company Inc., a worldwide leader in spices, has a famous slogan, "Think Twice for the Company and Once for Yourself and the Company Will Think Twice for the Employee and Once for Itself." (http://www.mccormick.com/content.cfm?ID=11285)
 • Owens & Minor Inc. is a worldwide distributor of medical supplies to hospitals. Its teamwork philosophy involves many stakeholders. (http://www.owens-minor.com/teammates/)
 • Johnson & Johnson, a Fortune Top 50 company, has a special section on its Web site about corporate social responsibility. (http://www.jnj.com/community/index.htm)

**Local Companies and Corporate Philosophy:** Ask the students to interview business leaders in their community to see whether their corporate philosophy matches that of Milton Friedman or John Mackey.

# VISUAL 9.1
# SUMMARY OF FRIEDMAN'S AND MACKEY'S VIEWS

|  | Friedman | Mackey |
|---|---|---|
| Role of *profit* | • Profit is the sole reason for the firm to exist.<br><br>• Profit provides incentives for efficiency and dynamic growth. It ultimately raises living standards by providing customers with goods and services they want. | • Profit is necessary for business survival, but other goals are also important to the firm.<br><br>• Profit provides incentives for efficiency and dynamic growth. It ultimately raises living standards by providing customers with goods and services they want. |
| Ethical duties | • Fiduciary duties of employees to *shareholders*<br><br>• Employees should follow all laws and treat people honestly, courteously and ethically. | • Fiduciary duties of employees to a wide range of stakeholders |
| Stakeholders (Duty owed) | • Shareholders only (profit) | • Customers (honesty, service, price)<br><br>• Team member or employees (honesty, reward, recognition)<br><br>• Shareholders (return on capital, profits, psychic income)<br><br>• Suppliers (honesty, loyalty, reward)<br><br>• Communities (giving 5 percent of profits to community causes)<br><br>• Environment (stewardship) |

## VISUAL 9.2
## THE INVISIBLE HAND

"[A merchant] intends only his own security; and by directing that industry in such a manner as its produce may be of the greatest value, he intends only his own gain, and he is in this, as in many other cases, led by an invisible hand to promote an end which was no part of his intention. Nor is it always the worse for the society that it was no part of it. By pursuing his own interest he frequently promotes that of the society more effectually than when he really intends to promote it. I have never known much good done by those who affected to trade for the public good."

— Adam Smith, *The Wealth of Nations*

eds. R.H. Campbell and A.S. Skinner (Indianapolis: Liberty Press, 1981 [1776]), 26-27

## Questions

**1.** What do you think Smith means when he says that a merchant who strives only for his own gain unwittingly promotes the interests of society? What are society's interests, and how does the merchant promote them?

**2.** Whose position on the social responsibility of business does Smith's quote support: Friedman's or Mackey's?

**3.** Do you agree or disagree with this statement by Adam Smith? Why?

## ACTIVITY 9.1
## TWO VIEWS ON THE SOCIAL RESPONSIBILITY
## OF BUSINESS

**Directions:** Read the articles below on the social responsibility of business. Then write the answers to the questions. Milton Friedman won the Nobel Prize in economic sciences in 1976. John Mackey is co-founder and chief executive officer of Whole Foods Market Inc.

**The Social Responsibility of Business Is to Increase Its Profits** (excerpt)
By Milton Friedman
*The New York Times Magazine*, September 13, 1970, 122-6
© 1970, Milton Friedman, reprinted with permission

Photo: © Nobelstiftelsen

When I hear businessmen speak eloquently about the "social responsibilities of business in a free-enterprise system," I am reminded of the wonderful line about the Frenchman who discovered at the age of 70 that he had been speaking prose all his life. The businessmen believe that they are defending free enterprise when they declaim that business is not concerned "merely" with profit but also with promoting desirable "social" ends; that business has a "social conscience" and takes seriously its responsibilities for providing employment, eliminating discrimination, avoiding pollution and whatever else may be the catchwords of the contemporary crop of reformers. In fact they are — or would be if they or anyone else took them seriously — preaching pure and unadulterated socialism. Businessmen who talk this way are unwitting puppets of the intellectual forces that have been undermining the basis of a free society these past decades.

The discussions of the "social responsibilities of business" are notable for their analytical looseness and lack of rigor. What does it mean to say that "business" has responsibilities? Only people can have responsibilities. A corporation is an artificial person and in this sense may have artificial responsibilities, but "business" as a whole cannot be said to have responsibilities, even in this vague sense. The first step toward clarity in examining the doctrine of the social responsibility of business is to ask precisely what it implies for whom.

Presumably, the individuals who are to be responsible are businessmen, which

## ACTIVITY 9.1 (continued)
## TWO VIEWS ON THE SOCIAL RESPONSIBILITY
## OF BUSINESS

means individual proprietors or corporate executives. Most of the discussion of social responsibility is directed at corporations, so in what follows I shall mostly neglect the individual proprietors and speak of corporate executives.

In a free-enterprise, private-property system, a corporate executive is an employee of the owners of the business. He has direct responsibility to his employers. That responsibility is to conduct the business in accordance with their desires, which generally will be to make as much money as possible while conforming to the basic rules of the society, both those embodied in law and those embodied in ethical custom. Of course, in some cases his employers may have a different objective. A group of persons might establish a corporation for an eleemosynary [charitable] purpose — for example, a hospital or a school. The manager of such a corporation will not have money profit as his objective but the rendering of certain services.

In either case, the key point is that, in his capacity as a corporate executive, the manager is the agent of the individuals who own the corporation or establish the eleemosynary institution, and his primary responsibility is to them.

Needless to say, this does not mean that it is easy to judge how well he is performing his task. But at least the criterion of performance is straightforward, and the persons among whom a voluntary contractual arrangement exists are clearly defined.

Of course, the corporate executive is also a person in his own right. As a person, he may have many other responsibilities that he recognizes or assumes voluntarily — to his family, his conscience, his feelings of charity, his church, his clubs, his city, his country. He may feel impelled by these responsibilities to devote part of his income to causes he regards as worthy, to refuse to work for particular corporations, even to leave his job, for example, to join his country's armed forces. If we wish, we may refer to some of these responsibilities as "social responsibilities." But in these respects he is acting as a principal, not an agent; he is spending his own money or time or energy, not the money of his employers or the time or energy he has contracted to devote to their purposes. If these are "social responsibilities," they are the social responsibilities of individuals, not of business . . . .

## ACTIVITY 9.1 (continued)
## TWO VIEWS ON THE SOCIAL RESPONSIBILITY
## OF BUSINESS

The difficulty of exercising "social responsibility" illustrates, of course, the great virtue of private competitive enterprise — it forces people to be responsible for their own actions and makes it difficult for them to "exploit" other people for either selfish or unselfish purposes. They can do good — but only at their own expense.

**Rethinking the Social Responsibility of Business: Putting Customers Ahead of Investors** (excerpt)
By John Mackey
*Reason* 37 no. 5, October 2005, 28-32. Reprinted with permission

Photo: Whole Foods Market

In 1970 Milton Friedman wrote that "there is one and only one social responsibility of business — to use its resources and engage in activities designed to increase its profits so long as it stays within the rules of the game, which is to say, engages in open and free competition without deception or fraud." That's the orthodox view among free market economists: that the only social responsibility a law-abiding business has is to maximize profits for the shareholders.

I strongly disagree. I'm a businessman and a free market libertarian, but I believe that the enlightened corporation should try to create value for all of its constituencies. From an investor's perspective, the purpose of the business is to maximize profits. But that's not the purpose for other stakeholders — for customers, employees, suppliers, and the community. Each of those groups will define the purpose of the business in terms of its own needs and desires, and each perspective is valid and legitimate.

My argument should not be mistaken for a hostility to profit. I believe I know something about creating shareholder value. When I co-founded Whole Foods Market 27 years ago, we began with $45,000 in capital; we only had $290,000 in sales our first year. During the last 12 months we had sales of more than $4.6 billion, net profits of more than $160 million, and a market capitalization over $8 billion.

## ACTIVITY 9.1 (continued)
## TWO VIEWS ON THE SOCIAL RESPONSIBILITY
## OF BUSINESS

But we have not achieved our tremendous increase in shareholder value by making shareholder value the primary purpose of our business. In my marriage, my wife's happiness is an end in itself, not merely a means to my own happiness; love leads me to put my wife's happiness first, but in doing so I also make myself happier. Similarly, the most successful businesses put the customer first, ahead of the investors. In the profit-centered business, customer happiness is merely a means to an end: maximizing profits. In the customer-centered business, customer happiness is an end in itself, and will be pursued with greater interest, passion, and empathy than the profit-centered business is capable of.

. . . At Whole Foods, we measure our success by how much value we can create for all six of our most important stakeholders: customers, team members (employees), investors, vendors, communities, and the environment . . . .

There is, of course, no magical formula to calculate how much value each stakeholder should receive from the company. It is a dynamic process that evolves with the competitive marketplace. No stakeholder remains satisfied for long. It is the function of company leadership to develop solutions that continually work for the common good.

Many thinking people will readily accept my arguments that caring about customers and employees is good business. But they might draw the line at believing a company has any responsibility to its community and environment. To donate time and capital to philanthropy, they will argue, is to steal from the investors . . . .

This position sounds reasonable. A company's assets do belong to the investors, and its management does have a duty to manage those assets responsibly. In my view, the argument is not wrong so much as it is too narrow.

First, there can be little doubt that a certain amount of corporate philanthropy is simply good business and works for the long-term benefit of the investors. ... That said, I believe such programs would be completely justifiable even if they produced no profits and no P.R. . . . .

## ACTIVITY 9.1 (continued)
## TWO VIEWS ON THE SOCIAL RESPONSIBILITY
## OF BUSINESS

The shareholders of a public company own their stock voluntarily. If they don't agree with the philosophy of the business, they can always sell their investment, just as the customers and employees can exit their relationships with the company if they don't like the terms of trade. If that is unacceptable to them, they always have the legal right to submit a resolution at our annual shareholders meeting to change the company's philanthropic philosophy. A number of our company policies have been changed over the years through successful shareholder resolutions.

Another objection to the Whole Foods philosophy is where to draw the line. If donating 5 percent of profits is good, wouldn't 10 percent be even better? Why not donate 100 percent of our profits to the betterment of society? But the fact that Whole Foods has responsibilities to our community doesn't mean that we don't have any responsibilities to our investors. It's a question of finding the appropriate balance and trying to create value for all of our stakeholders . . . .

**"If donating 5 percent of profits is good, wouldn't 10 percent be even better?"**

That doesn't answer the question of why we give money to the community stakeholder. For that, you should turn to one of the fathers of free-market economics, Adam Smith. *The Wealth of Nations* was a tremendous achievement, but economists would be well served to read Smith's other great book, *The Theory of Moral Sentiments*. There he explains that human nature isn't just about self-interest. It also includes sympathy, empathy, friendship, love, and the desire for social approval. As motives for human behavior, these are at least as important as self-interest. For many people, they are more important . . . .

The business model that Whole Foods has embraced could represent a new form of capitalism, one that more consciously works for the common good instead of depending solely on the "invisible hand" to generate positive results for society. The "brand" of capitalism is in terrible shape throughout the world, and corporations are widely seen as selfish, greedy, and uncaring. This is both unfortunate and unnecessary, and could be changed if businesses and economists widely adopted the business model that I have outlined here . . . .

## ACTIVITY 9.1 (continued)
## TWO VIEWS ON THE SOCIAL RESPONSIBILITY
## OF BUSINESS

### Questions

**1.** According to Milton Friedman, what is the responsibility of corporate executives?

**2.** Beyond making a profit, what ethical responsibilities does Friedman say businesses have to society in general?

**3.** Does Friedman's emphasis on maximizing corporate profits mean that he is not concerned with the welfare of society?

**4.** Why does Friedman believe a corporate executive should be socially responsible as an individual but not in his or her corporate role?

**5.** What is the difference between a shareholder and a stakeholder?

# ACTIVITY 9.1 (continued)
# TWO VIEWS ON THE SOCIAL RESPONSIBILITY
# OF BUSINESS

**6.** Who are the stakeholders in John Mackey's conception of the corporation? What ethical duties does the corporation owe to each stakeholder?

**7.** What motives besides money does Mackey argue are important in understanding human nature? How might these motives be relevant in running a business?

**8.** Are Mackey's views on the social responsibility of business inconsistent with maximizing profits? Why?

**9.** Corporations have provided billions of dollars in aid to victims of Hurricane Katrina, the South Pacific tsunami and AIDS in Africa. In some cases, these contributions have been more effective than government aid. Would Friedman and Mackey support these types of donations?

# Lesson 10 – What Is Economic Justice?

*The students play the Veil of Ignorance game to reveal how altering people's self-interest transforms their vision of economic justice.*

## OVERVIEW

### Economics
Economics has traditionally focused more on analyzing production and consumption than on assessing the fairness of economic outcomes. Yet economic justice is an important value to individuals and societies. Scarcity means that not all wants can be satisfied, and an economic system may generate a high degree of inequality. Some people see inequalities as an inevitable or desirable outcome of normal economic behavior. Others find the degree of economic inequality in today's society to be morally unacceptable.

### Ethics
In ethics, justice is the fair treatment of all people. Although it is difficult to define justice or fairness in a way that everyone would accept, there is widespread agreement that certain practices or outcomes are unfair. To determine if something is just, people ask two different — and possibly contradictory — questions:
  • Is the outcome or result fair?
  • Is the process fair?
People who emphasize outcomes tend to see the existing degree of economic inequality as morally wrong. People who emphasize process are more likely to approve the results of a system — even if the results are highly unequal — provided that individuals have equal opportunity to succeed.

## LESSON DESCRIPTION

In this lesson the students explore basic ideas of justice through a class discussion. Then they play the Veil of Ignorance game. In the first round of the game, groups of students get Role Cards and vote for a slate of economic policies according to the interests of their assigned role: a teacher, a retiree, a high-income executive, a college student or an unemployed person. After the vote, each group explains how and why it chose the policies it supported. In the second round, all the groups receive an identical Role Card with no age, gender or economic status. They must now operate behind a "veil of ignorance," a term developed by the philosopher John Rawls. The groups cast new votes on economic policies without being able to pursue their narrow interests because they don't know who they are. The lesson closes with a debriefing of the game.

## CONCEPTS

Economic inequality
Income
Fairness
Justice
Veil of ignorance
Wealth

## CONTENT STANDARDS

1.  Productive resources are limited. Therefore, people cannot have all the goods and services they want; as a result, they must choose some things and give up others.

3.  Different methods can be used to allocate goods and services. People, acting individually or collectively through government, must choose which methods to use to allocate different kinds of goods and services.

4.  People respond predictably to positive and negative incentives.

13. Income for most people is determined by the market value of the productive resources they sell. What workers earn depends, primarily, on the market value of what they produce and how productive they are.

16. There is an economic role for government in a market economy whenever the benefits of a government policy outweigh its costs. Governments often provide for national defense, address environmental concerns, define and protect property rights, and attempt to make markets more competitive. Most government policies also redistribute income.

## OBJECTIVES

The students will:
1. Explain why people disagree about what is just.

2. Contrast a just process with a just outcome.

3. Explain how individuals may seek their own interests through public policy.

4. Contrast self-interested economic behavior with behavior behind the "Veil of Ignorance."

## TIME REQUIRED

45 minutes

## MATERIALS

1. Visuals 10.1, 10.2, 10.3, 10.4 and 10.5

2. One Round 1 Role Card for each group, cut out from Activity 10.1

3. One Round 2 Role Card for each group, cut out from Activity 10.2

4. One copy of Activity 10.3 for each student

## PROCEDURE

1. Tell the students that they will play two rounds of a game that illustrates an important concept about justice. This concept is called the *veil of ignorance.*

2. Display Visual 10.1. Tell the students that economics hasn't traditionally focused on the *fairness* of economic outcomes — yet economic justice is an important value to individuals and societies. Remind the students of scarcity. Because of scarcity, not all wants can be satisfied — and people differ greatly in their abilities and opportunities to satisfy their wants.

3. Ask the students: Is it easier to define what is "fair" or to label an outcome as "unfair"? ***Labeling an outcome as "unfair" is easier. Fairness itself is hard to define.***

4. Explain that in ethics, justice is the fair treatment of all people. To determine if something is just, people ask two different — and possibly contradictory — questions:
   • Is the outcome or result fair?
   • Is the process fair?
Remind the students that a fair process may still generate highly unequal outcomes. Tell them that people who emphasize outcomes tend to see the existing degree of economic inequality as morally unjustifiable, while people who emphasize process tend to approve the results of a system — even if these results are highly unequal — provided that individuals have equal opportunity to succeed.

5. Ask the students: Do you think the competition on reality TV shows is fair? ***Accept a variety of answers. The outcome is unequal. The winners win large prizes while everyone else gets much smaller prizes or nothing at all, sometimes while being humiliated and even threatened physically. But the process is fair if the rules are fair and all the contestants follow them.***

6. Ask the students: Do you think it is fair that some students are admitted to higher-quality colleges and universities and other students are rejected? *Accept a variety of answers. The outcome is unequal. The process may or may not be fair, depending on the student's point of view.*

    *College admission depends on a number of factors including grades and test scores, and grades and test scores depend in part on intelligence and effort. However, families with higher incomes can pay for tutors and special classes to improve their children's grades and SAT scores and even for application consultants who can help their children "package" their grades, activities and accomplishment to make the children more appealing to certain schools. Other students may be admitted through affirmative action or because they are the children of alumni. This question involves both outcome and process issues.*

7. Display Visual 10.2. Read the directions for the Veil of Ignorance game, and ask the students if they have any questions.

## ROUND 1

8. Divide the students into five groups. The number of students in each group will depend on class size. Give each group one Role Card from Activity 10.1.

9. Give each student a copy of the Economic Policy Ballot (Activity 10.3). Remind the students that the groups will have to explain their votes at the end of Round 1.

10. Display Visual 10.3 and review Issue 1 on raising government revenue. For the progressive-income-tax option, show the students how to calculate the amount of tax a person would pay for a given level of income. Then discuss the flat-rate option of taxing everyone's income at the same 15-percent rate. Be sure to tell the stu-

dents that both options are expected to raise the same amount of revenue for the government.

11. Briefly go over the remaining policy issues: No. 2 on unemployment assistance, No. 3 on immigrant workers and No. 4 on health insurance.
    (**Note:** You may omit one or more issues or substitute your own topics instead.)

12. Allow the students several minutes to discuss the issues within their groups. Then instruct each group to mark Vote 1 of the Economic Policy Ballot on Activity 10.3. After voting is complete, ask each group to identify its role in society and family income and make a brief presentation that explains how the group voted and why. Write this information on Visual 10.4 in the appropriate place for each group.

## ROUND 2

13. Give each group one Role Card from Activity 10.2 to begin Round 2. Tell the students that they must now analyze policies "behind a veil of ignorance" because they don't know who they are. Their Role Card doesn't give them their age, family income or other characteristic. Make sure the students decide the issues behind a veil of ignorance and not from their perspective as a teenage high school student.

14. Allow the students several minutes to discuss the issues within their groups. Then instruct each group to mark Vote 2 on the Economic Policy Ballot. After voting is complete, ask each group to tell the class how it voted on each issue and why. As each group makes its presentation, fill in the group's vote on each issue.

15. Display Visual 10.5. Work with the students through the answers.
    **Question 1:** In the second round, you didn't know your role or position in life. How did this affect your views about these economic policy issues? *Accept a variety*

*of answers. Many students will say that they first made decisions based on narrow self-interest, but in the second round they were forced to consider a wider perspective. What seems fair from one perspective might seem unfair from another.*

*In Round 1, the unemployed person would favor more generous unemployment assistance. The executive would probably favor modest assistance because a more-generous plan would mean higher business taxes. The teacher and art student do not pay business taxes, so they might support more generous benefits. The retiree might want more government spending for retirees and medical care rather than for unemployment assistance.*

*Workers in the United States with low skill levels would suffer from having guest workers because this might prevent market wages from rising. The company executive, however, would likely support a guest-worker law because the executive could find new workers without raising wages as much, allowing output at the factory to expand. The retiree might also like to hire inexpensive labor to repair the house.*

*In regard to health insurance, people who currently have good access to health care because of their incomes or jobs would favor private health insurance. They would be more interested in the quality of care and doctor choice. Low-income individuals who don't have jobs or have jobs that don't pay health benefits have uncertain access to health care and would be more likely to favor national health insurance.*

*But behind a veil of ignorance, the students don't know if they have a high, middle or low income. In their new role, therefore, they likely wouldn't advocate any tax system that placed special burdens on the rich or the poor. Some students may say they*

*supported a progressive tax system as "insurance" against being poor and would be willing pay high taxes if they are rich. The important point is that the students recognize the veil of ignorance takes away their ability to seek narrowly self-interested policies.*

**Question 2:** After playing this game, do you think fairness in economic policy should be based on achieving equal outcomes in society or providing a process for equal opportunity? Why is it not always possible to have both? *Accept a variety of answers. Make sure the students understand that policies to achieve a fair outcome often destroy the fair process. For example, if all students always receive the same grade regardless of achievement, this creates an unfair process because some students will be rewarded for little effort and others will be penalized for greater effort. By the same analogy, the students should see that creating a fair process usually results in unequal outcomes. For example, sporting events have fair rules, but some teams win and some lose.*

*People don't need to make every choice at the extreme; some balance between fair outcomes and fair process is often desirable. Thus, society may require a minimum safety net of equal outcomes in some cases because the alternative is an unacceptably unfair process. For example, ensuring that poor children receive proper vision care (an outcome) allows the children to compete on terms that are more fair in the classroom (a process). Providing vision care makes the process — and the likely outcomes — of equal opportunity more fair.*

**Question 3:** Since it is not actually possible to live behind a veil of ignorance, what lessons did you learn about resolving economic policy issues? *The Veil of Ignorance game is a technique that forces us to consider a wider perspective than our own. Considering issues*

*from the perspective of another per-
son stretches our moral imagination.
Policy making is enriched and cooperation is more likely.*

## CLOSURE

16. Explain to the students that, in real life,
we do not have an Economic Policy Ballot
on which we can vote all our policy preferences. Instead, we have to choose candidates whose views are close to ours, recog-
nizing that there will not be a perfect fit.
Although it is difficult to define fairness
and justice, we sense that some things
are unfair. Remind the students that the
Veil of Ignorance game shows the value of
assuming you don't know anything about
your station in life. The veil of ignorance
brings new insight about policies that
would be fair.

**The bottom line:** By pretending they're
behind the veil of ignorance, the students can
see how an understanding of fairness can arise
without regard to their own personal interests.

## ASSESSMENT

### Multiple-Choice Questions

10.1 Which of the following terms best
describes the situation in which people in a
society have large differences in incomes?
   A. Ethnic diversity
   *B. Economic inequality*
   C. Income unfairness
   D. Material inequity

10.2 Who is most likely to be upset when an
open society with good access to education
and jobs generates extreme differences in
income among its members?
   A. People who view justice in terms of
process
   *B. People who view justice in terms
of outcomes*
   C. People who view justice as
indefinable
   D. People who view justice as the
presence of freedom

10.3 What is the point of imagining the
choices you would make behind a veil of
ignorance?
   A. People tend to make poor choices
when they do not have enough
information.
   B. People tend to make good choices
because ignorance is easily swept away
through education.
   C. People tend to make fair choices
when they know the most about their own
personal situations and opportunities.
   *D. People tend to make fair choices
when they know so little that they cannot seek their own self-interest.*

### Essay Questions

10.1 Consider the following statement:
"International statistics show that there is
more inequality of incomes in the United
States than in Sweden. These statistics
mean that Sweden is a more just society
than the United States." Write a brief
paragraph in favor of this statement
and another brief paragraph opposing it.
*Paragraphs favoring the statement
should emphasize an understanding
of inequality : that incomes are very
different and therefore living standards vary widely. Most paragraphs
opposing the statement will reflect a
view that equality of opportunity matters more than equality of outcomes.
Some students may argue that the statistics are not comparable.*

10.2 Suppose a physical education teacher has
a limited number of bonus points to award
in class. The teacher can allocate them in
one of two ways:
   • Disproportionately to the few students who most quickly run a difficult
obstacle course
   • Evenly to all the students who work
hard on completing the course, even if
they're not the fastest and may not finish
   How do you think the teacher should
award the points? First answer this question from your own self-interested situa-

tion (knowing your own athletic abilities). Then explain what your answer would be behind a veil of ignorance. *Accept all answers. The key is to see whether the students have developed a deeper appreciation for what is fair by placing themselves behind the veil of ignorance.*

## GOING FURTHER

**Controversy about the Veil of Ignorance:** John Rawls, the philosopher who wrote about the veil of ignorance, died in 2002. His work was influential, but his ideas are still controversial. See the conflicting obituaries in the British newspaper *The Guardian* (http://www.guardian.co.uk/obitu-aries/story/0,3604,848488,00.html) and the journal *Liberty* (http://libertyunbound.com/archive/2003_02/narveson-rawls.html).

### Read More About Rawls' Work
• Advanced classes may be interested in reading John Rawls' work. His massive original book is *A Theory of Justice* (1971), but a shorter, 200-page paperback version is *Justice as Fairness: A Restatement* (Cambridge: Harvard University Press, 2001). Even with the restatement, Rawls is not easy going for most students.

• An easier book for advanced students is Thomas Sowell's *The Quest for Cosmic Justice* (New York: The Free Press, 1999). This book advocates fairness in rules and process rather than in outcomes.

**What People Earn:** *Parade* magazine, a supplement to many Sunday newspapers, has an annual survey of "What People Earn." For the survey's excellent interactive game, go to http://whatpeopleearn.parade.com

## VISUAL 10.1
## FAIRNESS AND JUSTICE

In recent years, economics has focused on economic efficiency, yet economic justice is also an important value to individuals and societies.

Because of scarcity, not all wants can be satisfied — and people differ greatly in their abilities and opportunities to satisfy their wants.

Is it easier to define what is "fair" or to label an outcome as "unfair"?

In ethics, *justice* is the fair treatment of everyone. To determine if something is just, people ask two different — and possibly contradictory — questions:
- Is the outcome or result fair?
- Is the process fair?

People who emphasize outcomes tend to see the existing degree of *economic inequality* as morally unjustifiable.

People who emphasize process tend to approve the results of a system, even if these results are highly unequal, provided that individuals have equal opportunity to succeed.

VISUAL 10.2
THE VEIL OF IGNORANCE GAME

**Directions:** This role-playing game will help you understand an important principle of justice. You will play the game in groups.

## Round 1

In this round, each group will receive a Role Card describing the position the group members occupy in society. Each group will determine which economic policies would benefit them personally. Then the members of the group will vote for these policies on an Economic Policy Ballot. This is Vote 1. After voting is complete, each group will identify its role in society and its income and make a brief presentation to the class that explains how it voted on each issue and why.

## Round 2

In the second round, each group will receive a new Role Card. The groups will discuss the issues and then vote again. This is Vote 2. After voting is complete, each group will briefly tell the class how it voted on each issue and why.

# VISUAL 10.3
# ISSUE 1: RAISING GOVERNMENT REVENUE

## OPTION A: PROGRESSIVE INCOME TAX
People with higher incomes pay a higher marginal tax rate.

| Annual Income | Tax Rate |
|---|---|
| Up to $ 10,000 | 0% |
| $ 10,001 to $ 50,000 | 10% |
| $ 50,001 to $100,000 | 20% |
| $100,001 to $300,000 | 30% |
| Over $300,000 | 50% |

Example: Jody earns $80,000 a year. Under a progressive tax rate:
- Jody pays 0% tax on the first $10,000 she earns   $10,000 x .0 = $      0
- Jody pays 10% tax on the next $40,000 she earns   $40,000 x .1 = $  4,000
- Jody pays 20% tax on the final $30,000 she earns   $30,000 x .2 = $  6,000

Jody's total tax on $80,000 income is   $0 + $4,000 + $6,000 = **$10,000**

## OPTION B: FLAT INCOME TAX
Everyone who receives an income pays the same tax rate of 15 percent. Under this plan, Jody would pay 15 percent of $80,000, or $12,000.

Options A and B are expected to raise identical amounts of tax revenue, even through individual families may pay different amounts of taxes under each option.

# VISUAL 10.4
# ECONOMIC POLICY BALLOT

**Group 1:** Role _____ Family Income _____

**Group 2:** Role _____ Family Income _____

**Group 3:** Role _____ Family Income _____

**Group 4:** Role _____ Family Income _____

**Group 5:** Role _____ Family Income _____

| | Vote 1<br>**Role and Income Known**<br>(Choose one policy for each issue) | | Vote 2<br>**Behind a Veil of Ignorance**<br>(Choose one policy for each issue) | |
|---|---|---|---|---|
| **Issue 1: Raising Government Revenue** | | | | |
| Group 1 | ☐ Progressive tax | ☐ Flat tax | ☐ Progressive tax | ☐ Flat tax |
| Group 2 | ☐ Progressive tax | ☐ Flat tax | ☐ Progressive tax | ☐ Flat tax |
| Group 3 | ☐ Progressive tax | ☐ Flat tax | ☐ Progressive tax | ☐ Flat tax |
| Group 4 | ☐ Progressive tax | ☐ Flat tax | ☐ Progressive tax | ☐ Flat tax |
| Group 5 | ☐ Progressive tax | ☐ Flat tax | ☐ Progressive tax | ☐ Flat tax |
| **Issue 2: Unemployment Assistance** | | | | |
| Group 1 | ☐ Modest | ☐ Generous | ☐ Modest | ☐ Generous |
| Group 2 | ☐ Modest | ☐ Generous | ☐ Modest | ☐ Generous |
| Group 3 | ☐ Modest | ☐ Generous | ☐ Modest | ☐ Generous |
| Group 4 | ☐ Modest | ☐ Generous | ☐ Modest | ☐ Generous |
| Group 5 | ☐ Modest | ☐ Generous | ☐ Modest | ☐ Generous |
| **Issue 3: Immigrant Workers** | | | | |
| Group 1 | ☐ Guest workers | ☐ Stronger law | ☐ Guest workers | ☐ Stronger law |
| Group 2 | ☐ Guest workers | ☐ Stronger law | ☐ Guest workers | ☐ Stronger law |
| Group 3 | ☐ Guest workers | ☐ Stronger law | ☐ Guest workers | ☐ Stronger law |
| Group 4 | ☐ Guest workers | ☐ Stronger law | ☐ Guest workers | ☐ Stronger law |
| Group 5 | ☐ Guest workers | ☐ Stronger law | ☐ Guest workers | ☐ Stronger law |
| **Issue 4: Health Insurance** | | | | |
| Group 1 | ☐ Private | ☐ National | ☐ Private | ☐ National |
| Group 2 | ☐ Private | ☐ National | ☐ Private | ☐ National |
| Group 3 | ☐ Private | ☐ National | ☐ Private | ☐ National |
| Group 4 | ☐ Private | ☐ National | ☐ Private | ☐ National |
| Group 5 | ☐ Private | ☐ National | ☐ Private | ☐ National |

VISUAL 10.5
QUESTIONS ABOUT THE VEIL OF IGNORANCE

**1.** In the second round, you didn't know your role or position in life. How did this affect your views about these economic policy issues?

**2.** After playing this game, do you think fairness in economic policy should be based on achieving equal outcomes in society or providing a process for equal opportunity? Why is it not always possible to have both?

**3.** Since it is not actually possible to live behind a veil of ignorance, what lessons did you learn about resolving economic policy issues?

# ACTIVITY 10.1
# ROUND 1 ROLE CARDS

| | |
|---|---|
| **Group 1** Role Card<br>**Unemployed laborer**<br><br>Years of education: **10**<br>Family income this year: **$8,000**<br>Total wealth (all assets): **$3,000**<br>Age: **28** | You are an unemployed day laborer. Your skill level is low because you dropped out of high school to work and help your mother make ends meet. Because of a slowdown in the construction industry, you were laid off two months ago and have not found another job. You do not have health insurance. You would like to find steady work and settle down. |
| **Group 2** Role Card<br>**Teacher**<br><br>Years of education: **16**<br>Family income this year: **$100,000**<br>Total wealth (all assets): **$150,000**<br>Age: **40** | You are a middle school music teacher. You are married and your spouse also works. Your spouse's income is $60,000 a year, and you make $40,000 a year, so your family income is $100,000. You have two children. If possible, you would like to start a college fund for your kids and move into a larger house. But tuition and housing prices are rising. |
| **Group 3** Role Card<br>**College art student**<br><br>Years of education: **12**<br>Family income this year: **$0**<br>Total wealth (all assets): **$2,000**<br>Age: **19** | You are a first-year student at a state college. You have two sisters and one brother, all younger than you. Your parents can support you for one more year, then they will expect you to pay all your own expenses by working. Eventually you would like to get a master's degree in art history and work in a museum. |

# ACTIVITY 10.1 (continued)
# ROUND 1 ROLE CARDS

**Group 4** Role Card
**Business executive**

Years of education: **18**
Family income this year: **$450,000**
Total wealth (all assets): **$2,500,000**
Age: **54**

You have worked your way up the corporate ladder and are now responsible for running a division in the XYZ Company with a large factory and annual sales of $300 million. You typically work 12 hours a day and must travel for extended periods. The factory employs 2,000 people, many of them in unskilled jobs. It is difficult to find new workers in your region without substantially raising wages. You would like to become the company president some day.

**Group 5** Role Card
**Retiree**

Years of education: **12**
Family income this year: **$50,000**
Total wealth (all assets): **$350,000**
Age: **68**

You retired three years ago from your job as a steelworker. You are able to live well off Social Security and a company pension. However, your assets are tied up in your house, for which you still make mortgage payments. The house badly needs repairs, but the cost of labor in your area is high. Your spouse is two years older than you and needs expensive medicines every month.

# ACTIVITY 10.2
# ROUND 2 ROLE CARDS (ALL GROUPS)

**Group 1** Role Card

Age: **Unknown**
Gender: **Unknown**
Occupation: **Unknown**
Family income this year: **Unknown**
Value of assets: **Unknown**
Marital status: **Unknown**

**Group 2** Role Card

Age: **Unknown**
Gender: **Unknown**
Occupation: **Unknown**
Family income this year: **Unknown**
Value of assets: **Unknown**
Marital status: **Unknown**

**Group 3** Role Card

Age: **Unknown**
Gender: **Unknown**
Occupation: **Unknown**
Family income this year: **Unknown**
Value of assets: **Unknown**
Marital status: **Unknown**

# ACTIVITY 10.2 (continued)
# ROUND 2 ROLE CARDS (ALL GROUPS)

**Group 4** Role Card

Age: **Unknown**
Gender: **Unknown**
Occupation: **Unknown**
Family income this year: **Unknown**
Value of assets: **Unknown**
Marital status: **Unknown**

**Group 5** Role Card

Age: **Unknown**
Gender: **Unknown**
Occupation: **Unknown**
Family income this year: **Unknown**
Value of assets: **Unknown**
Marital status: **Unknown**

# ACTIVITY 10.3
# ECONOMIC POLICY BALLOT

**Directions:** After the first round of group discussion based on your first Role Card, mark your ballot in the Vote 1 column according to your own best interests. After the second round of discussion based on your second Role Card, mark your ballot in the Vote 2 column according to your own best interests.

| Policy and Description<br>(Choose one policy for each issue) | Vote 1<br>Role and<br>Income Known | Vote 2<br>Behind a Veil<br>of Ignorance |
|---|---|---|
| **Issue 1: Raising Government Revenue** | | |
| **Progressive Income Tax:** People with higher family incomes pay a higher marginal tax rate. | Progressive tax | Progressive tax |
| **Flat Tax:** 15% tax rate on all incomes | Flat tax | Flat tax |
| **Issue 2: Unemployment Assistance** | | |
| **Modest Assistance:** Unemployed workers get 12 weeks of support while they search for a job. Taxes on businesses pay for assistance. | Modest | Modest |
| **Generous Assistance:** Unemployed workers get 24 weeks of support and job training while they search for work. Taxes on businesses pay for assistance. | Generous | Generous |
| **Issue 3: Immigrant Workers** | | |
| **Guest-Worker Law:** Law allows firms and households to hire immigrant workers in the United States without requiring U.S. citizenship. | Guest workers | Guest workers |
| **Stronger Immigration Law:** Stronger law makes it harder to hire certain immigrants by creating severe fines for firms and households that hire workers in the United States who do not have U.S. citizenship. | Stronger law | Stronger law |
| **Issue 4: Health Insurance** | | |
| **Private Insurance:** People buy health insurance on their own, choosing coverage and doctors. People without health insurance receive little health care. | Private | Private |
| **National Insurance:** Every citizen receives a standard level of health care defined by the government and paid for by taxes. Choice of doctors and coverage is restricted. | National | National |

# Test Bank

## MULTIPLE-CHOICE QUESTIONS

**1.1**  Researchers in economics
   A. face ethical issues only in normative economics.
   B. face ethical issues only in positive economics.
   C. face ethical issues in both positive and normative economics.
   D. face no ethical issues because economics is a science.

**1.2**  A moral hazard arises when a researcher
   A. is put in peril from dangerous workplace materials.
   B. has an economic incentive to behave unethically.
   C. is in jeopardy from being overly ethical.
   D. cannot behave ethically because of a legal restriction.

**1.3**  If productive resources are limited, scarcity implies that
   A. people will collect only the facts they consider most important.
   B. people will base their collection of facts solely on objective considerations.
   C. all facts are of equal importance to researchers.
   D. researchers don't consider values when they collect facts.

**2.1**  A game people use frequently for economic and psychological investigation is called the Ultimatum Game because the game
   A. shows how sellers operate when their product is the best in the market.
   B. is the ultimate in simplicity — that is, the simplest possible two-step game.
   C. involves a take-it-or-leave-it offer from one person to another.
   D. shows how disregarding the feelings of others generates profits.

**2.2**  The difference between rational self-interest and greed is that greed
   A. is excessive, while rational self-interest is a legitimate motivation for people.
   B. involves money but rational self-interest does not.
   C. exists only in a market system.
   D. concerns only consumers, while rational self-interest concerns consumers and producers.

**2.3**  Carol buys stock in a new technology company. The company grows, hires more employees and increases profits. Carol sells her stock for much more than she paid for it. This is an example of a
   A. zero-sum game.
   B. negative-sum game.
   C. positive-sum game.
   D. ultimatum game.

3.1 Markets are more efficient when the following characteristics are present:
  A. Economic actors are self-interested.
  B. Market activities are transparent.
  C. Economic actors uphold ethical standards of behavior.
  D. All of the above

3.2 A company board of directors hires a chief financial officer to carry out activities on behalf of the stockholders. This situation reflects
  A. a corporate hazard.
  B. fiduciary duty.
  C. ideology.
  D. none of the above.

3.3 Frank learns that an inherited genetic disease affects people in his family. This disease will likely cause early death. Frank immediately applies for a large life-insurance policy without disclosing this genetic fact. This situation
  A. is economically efficient because Frank gets to buy the insurance he wants.
  B. is economically efficient because Frank's family will need the money when he dies.
  C. is economically inefficient because of asymmetric information.
  D. is economically inefficient because of a fiduciary relationship.

4.1 Competitive markets promote all of the following behaviors except
  A. tolerating the values and opinions of customers.
  B. using force to achieve economic progress.
  C. providing incentives for individuals to serve other people.
  D. encouraging individuals to discipline themselves.

4.2 Even if no laws require it, business owners have an economic incentive to be tolerant when they hire employees and serve customers because of
  A. their religious views.
  B. their fear of major lawsuits.
  C. the Occupational Safety and Health Administration.
  D. the profit motive.

4.3 In *The Wealth of Nations*, economist Adam Smith argued that people can help others by helping themselves. His term for this idea was
  A. the social-service paradox.
  B. benevolent dictator.
  C. the invisible hand.
  D. enlightened self-absorption.

5.1 Based on "Moral Criticisms of Markets," which of the following statements would Paul Heyne support?
  A. Markets promote selfish behavior.
  B. Markets promote social cooperation among strangers.
  C. People do everything for money.
  D. Competition corrupts society.

**5.2**   Which of the following statements is a moral criticism of markets?
  A. Markets promote an inefficient allocation of resources.
  B. Market transactions are voluntary.
  C. Markets are more coercive than governments.
  D. Markets may corrupt civic virtues.

**5.3**   Which of the following allocation methods is most efficient and most responsive to the preferences of consumers who have income to spend?
  A. First-come/first-served
  B. Markets
  C. Government
  D. A lottery

**6.1**   Which of the following is NOT a characteristic of sweatshops?
  A. Sweatshops are workplaces that always earn high profits.
  B. Sweatshops are factories where people work long hours under unhealthy or unsafe working conditions.
  C. Sweatshops are workplaces where people can be subjected to intimidation and violence.
  D. Sweatshops are workplaces that do not treat workers with dignity.

**6.2**   Sweatshop conditions are often said to result from
  A. a transparent working environment in which outsiders can monitor conditions.
  B. the tendency of people to work together, no matter how bad the conditions may be.
  C. a large rural population, heavy population density and high rates of poverty.
  D. the tropical climate of some workplaces.

**6.3**   According to an economic view, exploitation is a condition that arises in what type of labor market?
  A. Markets with a lot of competition
  B. Markets with fewer workers than the number of available jobs
  C. Markets with many employers
  D. Markets with little competition

**7.1**   Which of these statements about a price ceiling is correct?
  A. A price ceiling causes a shortage if the ceiling price is above the equilibrium price.
  B. A price ceiling causes a surplus if the ceiling price is above the equilibrium price.
  C. A price ceiling causes a shortage if the ceiling price is below the equilibrium price.
  D. A price ceiling shifts the demand curve to the right.

**7.2**   If a legal market in kidneys for transplant replaced the current law forbidding the buying and selling of kidneys, what would happen?
  A. The price would rise, and the quantity of kidneys demanded would increase.
  B. The price would rise, and the quantity of kidneys supplied would increase.
  C. The shortage of transplant kidneys would increase.
  D. The supply curve for transplant kidneys would shift to the right.

**7.3** Which ethical theory would be most supportive of a legal, open market for kidneys?
    **A.** Outcomes-based ethics
    **B.** Duty-based ethics
    **C.** Virtue-based ethics
    **D.** Value-based ethics

**8.1** What welfare goal is allocative efficiency based on?
    **A.** The satisfaction of individual consumer preferences
    **B.** The greatest happiness for the poorest members of society
    **C.** Saving the most lives
    **D.** Being fair to all citizens

**8.2** Joan received a birthday gift of an expensive pink sweater. She hates pink and would prefer to return the sweater to the store and use the money for dinner and a movie. From Joan's perspective, the current allocation of goods is
    **A.** efficient because people should treasure the gifts they receive.
    **B.** efficient because Joan hasn't yet returned the sweater.
    **C.** inefficient because the gift was from a family member.
    **D.** inefficient because it doesn't satisfy Joan's preferences.

**8.3** An economic policy could create economic efficiency but might not be fair. To resolve this problem requires the use of
    **A.** aggregate economics.
    **B.** normative economics.
    **C.** inflation economics.
    **D.** positive economics.

**9.1** Which of the following is true of fiduciary duties?
    **A.** They are very unprofitable.
    **B.** They bind employees to an expectation of honesty and loyalty to the employer.
    **C.** Employees must adhere to them, but not employers.
    **D.** Employers must adhere to them, but not employees.

**9.2** According to John Mackey,
    **A.** a company has an ethical duty only to its shareholders.
    **B.** achieving short-run profits is a company's principal goal.
    **C.** communities have obligations to employers.
    **D.** businesses have obligations to community stakeholders.

**9.3** According to Milton Friedman,
    **A.** businesses should share their profits with customers and the community.
    **B.** neither individuals nor businesses have a social responsibility beyond making profits.
    **C.** a company executive has a direct responsibility only to the company's owners (shareholders).
    **D.** maximizing profits is not consistent with improving the welfare of society.

**10.1** Which of the following terms best describes the situation in which people in a society have large differences in incomes?

    **A.** Ethnic diversity

    **B.** Economic inequality

    **C.** Income unfairness

    **D.** Material inequity

**10.2** Who is most likely to be upset when an open society with good access to education and jobs generates extreme differences in income among its members?

    **A.** People who view justice in terms of process

    **B.** People who view justice in terms of outcomes

    **C.** People who view justice as indefinable

    **D.** People who view justice as the presence of freedom

**10.3** What is the point of imagining the choices you would make behind a veil of ignorance?

    **A.** People tend to make poor choices when they do not have enough information.

    **B.** People tend to make good choices because ignorance is easily swept away through education.

    **C.** People tend to make fair choices when they know the most about their own personal situations and opportunities.

    **D.** People tend to make fair choices when they know so little that they cannot seek their own self-interest.

## ESSAY QUESTIONS

**1.1** In what ways are facts different from values? In what ways are they related in economic research?

**1.2** What absolute moral values are necessary to conduct scientific research?

**2.1** One winter the weather is unusually cold, and a fuel-oil dealer finds that customers are ordering much more heating oil. If the dealer raises prices in response, is this an example of rational self-interest or greed? Support your answer.

**2.2** When driving on the freeway, Carl blows his horn repeatedly, tailgates cars and cuts in front of them if he can. Carl explains, "Other drivers are in my way, and I operate the way I do to get to my destination sooner." What benefits does Carl receive from driving in this manner? What costs does he incur? Is Carl showing rational self-interest or greed? Does Carl's strategy always work?

**3.1** Analyze the extent and impact of fiduciary conduct in the operation of business.

**3.2** Analyze how transparency affects the efficiency of markets. In markets that lack transparency, what role does ethical conduct play?

**4.1** In the early 1940s, professional baseball, like much of American society, was characterized by rigid racial segregation. Several baseball club owners were convinced that African-Americans should not play in the major leagues. But in 1947 club owner Branch Rickey brought Jackie Robinson up from the minor leagues to play for the Brooklyn Dodgers. A few years later many African-American players joined major league teams. Why do you suppose Branch Rickey took the risk to sign Jackie Robinson?

**4.2** You are the manager of a new boutique coffee shop and art gallery called Frame of Mind. Your immediate task is to complete the training of your three new employees. You have already shown them how to prepare the different coffee drinks, and you have helped them become familiar with the artwork in the gallery and the artists whose work is on display. Now you need to train the employees on the importance of good customer service. Identify and explain two values that you will stress to ensure good customer service and foster positive behavior on the part of your employees.

**5.1** Karl Marx was the major proponent of communism (central planning by the government). A famous paraphrase of Marx is: "From each according to ability; to each according to need." Explain this quotation using moral theory. Do you think Marx was correct in condemning market activities?

**5.2** List and explain the moral limitations of markets. Explain why you agree or disagree with these limits.

**6.1** Do sweatshops prove that firms exploit workers in developing countries? Why?

**6.2** Analyze the advantages and disadvantages of three policy options regarding sweatshops. Which solution do you favor and why?

**7.1** Analyze the impact of the current federal law, which prohibits the sale of kidneys and allows only free-will donations.

**7.2** Before it was stopped, bidding for a kidney on eBay reached $5.7 million. Without considering the fact that buying kidneys is illegal, do you think the bidding should have been stopped?

**8.1** What do modern economists mean by welfare and allocative efficiency? How do economists apply these concepts to public-policy analysis? What problems exist with the use of these concepts?

**8.2** There are 10 people and space for only five in a life raft. How would you decide which people get a place on the raft? What solution to this problem would economists consider allocatively efficient? What other values besides efficiency are important in analyzing this situation?

**9.1** Compare and contrast the views of Milton Friedman and John Mackey on corporate social responsibility. Which view do you find more compelling and why?

**9.2** Imagine that you are the CEO of a corporation. The mayor of the city where your corporate offices are located asks your corporation for a major donation to build a new community park and swimming pool. How would you respond? Explain your answer.

**10.1** Consider the following statement: "International statistics show that there is more inequality of incomes in the United States than in Sweden. These statistics mean that Sweden is a more just society than the United States." Write a brief paragraph in favor of this statement and another brief paragraph opposing it.

**10.2** Suppose a physical education teacher has a limited number of bonus points to award in class. The teacher can allocate them in one of two ways:
  • Disproportionately to the few students who most quickly run a difficult obstacle course
  • Evenly to all the students who work hard on completing the course, even if they're not the fastest and may not finish

How do you think the teacher should award the points? First answer this question from your own self-interested situation (knowing your own athletic abilities). Then explain what your answer would be behind a veil of ignorance.

# Glossary of Terms

**Accountability:** assuming responsibility for one's actions (Lesson 4)

**Allocative efficiency:** a situation in which consumer preferences are maximized; it is not possible to make one person better off without making someone else worse off; a situation in which consumers are able to obtain the goods and services that best satisfy their individual preferences, given their income constraints (Lesson 8)

**Asymmetric information:** a situation in which one person in a transaction has more information than the other person (Lesson 3)

**Character:** intentions and conduct relating to virtue (Lesson 3)

**Civic virtue:** actions in the public arena that promote positive externalities (Lesson 5)

**Coercion:** the use of power to produce a non-voluntary exchange; taking unfair advantage of others (Lesson 5)

**Competition:** a situation of many independent buyers and sellers in which no single participant can influence the market price (Lessons 3, 5 and 6)

**Consumer welfare:** the analysis of gains or losses to buyers; the ability of an economy to satisfy individual consumer preferences (Lesson 8)

**Cooperation:** action undertaken through voluntary collective effort (Lesson 4)

**Corruption:** granting a public favor for pay or other remuneration (Lesson 5)

**Courtesy:** consideration of others (Lesson 4)

**Demand:** quantity of a good or service that buyers are willing and able to buy at all possible prices during a period of time (Lesson 7)

**Discipline:** control of one's emotions or actions (Lesson 4)

**Discrimination:** valuing or treating people unequally (Lesson 4)

**Duty:** obligations to oneself or others (Lesson 3)

**Duty-based ethics:** a moral philosophy that discerns right or wrong based on the analysis of one's obligations (Lessons 6 and 7)

**Economic inequality:** a situation in which the distribution of income or wealth differs within a group; a situation in which people in a society have large differences in incomes (Lesson 10)

**Economic model:** a simplified picture of reality which hypothesizes causality between variables in order to predict or understand outcomes (Lesson 1)

**Economics:** the study of how society deals with scarcity (Introduction)

**Efficiency:** achieving a goal most effectively; in economics, achieving the goals of productive and allocative efficiency (Lesson 5)

**Enlightened self-interest:** considering the needs of others as a means of enhancing one's own well-being (Lesson 3)

**Enterprise:** risk-taking and strength of effort (Lesson 4)

**Equilibrium price:** the value at which the quantity demanded equals the quantity supplied in a market (Lesson 7)

**Ethics:** the study of right and wrong actions (Introduction)

**Exploitation:** paying a worker less than the marginal value produced (Lesson 6)

**Facts:** knowledge about the world (Lesson 1)

**Fairness:** a concern for equal outcome or equal opportunity (Lessons 2 and 10)

**Fiduciary duty:** the obligation of one party to another party; a situation in which trust is expected (Lessons 1, 3 and 9)

**Greed:** excessive desire for something (Lesson 2)

**Gresham's Law:** a theorem that posits that only one form of commodity money can circulate in the long run because weaker money will drive out the stronger money; the thesis can be used to posit that only one type of labor or environmental regulations can exist in the same market because weaker regulators will drive out stronger ones (Lesson 6)

**Honesty:** truthfulness (Lesson 4)

**Human rights:** a concern for the inherent dignity, worth and essential liberties of individuals (Lesson 6)

**Ideology:** a framework of beliefs or theories about the world (Lesson 1)

**Incentives:** rewards and penalties that affect behavior (Lessons 3, 4, 7 and 8)

**Income:** earnings over a time period, such as a year (Lesson 10)

**Invisible hand:** Adam Smith's idea that humans are guided by instincts, which in the right institutional setting will produce a harmonious order (Lesson 4)

**Justice:** A concern for fairness in outcomes or in rules and opportunities; the fair treatment of everyone (Lessons 6 and 10)

**Market:** a mechanism that brings buyers and sellers together to facilitate exchange (Lessons 4 and 5)

**Moral hazard:** a situation in which one party to a transaction has both an incentive and the ability to extract unearned rewards from another party or behave unethically (Lessons 1 and 3)

**Normative economics:** the study of what is most desirable, requiring value judgments (Lessons 1 and 8)

**Outcomes-based ethics:** a moral philosophy that discerns right or wrong action based on the consequences produced by the action (Lessons 6 and 7)

**Positive economics:** the study of facts and theories about the way the world works (Lessons 1 and 8)

**Price ceiling:** a maximum legal price (Lesson 7)

**Principal-agent agreement:** a contract in which an owner employs a manager or employee with expectations of fiduciary behavior (Lesson 9)

**Productive efficiency:** achieving maximum output for a minimum of input (Lesson 8)

**Profit:** the reward to entrepreneurs or business owners; what is left after all other costs have been covered (Lesson 9)

**Prudence:** appropriate regard to one's own safety and well-being (Lesson 2)

**Rational behavior:** actions that consistently enable a person to achieve a goal (Lesson 2)

**Responsibility:** upholding one's duties and obligations to oneself and others (Lesson 4)

**Scarcity:** a situation of wants exceeding limited resources (Lesson 5)

**Self-interest:** concern for one's own safety and well-being (Lessons 2, 3, 4 and 5)

**Shareholder:** a person with ownership rights to a firm (Lesson 9)

**Social responsibility of business:** the idea that for-profit firms have obligations beyond shareholders to communities, workers or others (Lesson 9)

**Specialization:** focusing on producing a few things, as opposed to making all things (Lesson 1)

**Stakeholder:** a person, firm or community affected by a business (Lesson 9)

**Supply:** the amount of a good or service that producers are willing and able to offer for sale at each possible price during a given period of time (Lesson 7)

**Tolerance:** openness to or acceptance of differences (Lesson 4)

**Values:** principles or beliefs that guide behavior and choice (Lesson 1)

**Veil of ignorance:** a technique used by philosopher John Rawls to discern rules of justice (Lesson 10)

**Virtue-based ethics:** a moral philosophy that discerns right or wrong based on whether one's actions contribute to the formation of good character (Lessons 6 and 7)

**Wealth:** accumulated assets owned at a point in time (Lesson 10)

**Welfare economics:** the evaluation of an economic system based on how well it maximizes the well-being of its people (Lesson 8)